《论语》名句故事

THE ANALECTS STORIES

孔子学院总部赠送
Donated by Confucius Institute Headquarters

图书在版编目（CIP）数据

《论语》名句故事：汉英对照 / 山东美猴动漫文化艺术传媒有限公司编著；窦芳霞译. —— 北京：五洲传播出版社，2014.7
ISBN 978-7-5085-2779-6

Ⅰ.①论… Ⅱ.①山… ②窦… Ⅲ.①漫画 – 作品集 – 中国 – 现代 Ⅳ.① J228.2

中国版本图书馆 CIP 数据核字（2014）第 122518 号

山东美猴动漫文化艺术传媒有限公司　编著

策　　划：陈洪庆
主　　编：周永祥
艺术指导：李作义
英文翻译：窦芳霞
统　　筹：熊雯璐
责任编辑：董　宇
助理编辑：董　智

《论语》名句故事

出　　版：五洲传播出版社
发　　行：五洲传播出版社
地　　址：北京市海淀区北三环中路 31 号凯奇大厦 7 层
邮政编码：100088
电　　话：010-82007837，82001477，82003137
制版单位：北京锦绣圣艺文化发展有限公司
印　　刷：北京一步飞印刷有限公司
开　　本：889mm×1094mm 1/16
印　　张：11
版　　次：2014 年 7 月第 1 版 2014 年 7 月第 1 次印刷
书　　号：ISBN 978-7-5085-2779-6
定　　价：68.00 元

004
有教无类 Educate All People Without Discrimination
014
见贤思齐 Try to Emulate Him When You See a Good Man
025
人而无信 不知其可 If a Man Does not Keep His Word, What is He Good for?
033
温故而知新 Gain New Knowledge by Reviewing Old
040
钓而不钢 弋不射宿 Fish Without a Fishnet and Hunt Without Shooting at Animals that are Sleeping
050
节用而爱人 Be Economical and Love People
056
父母在 不远游 Don't Travel Far from Home if Parents are still Living
063
知之为知之 Knowing is Knowing
072
惠而不费 Doing Favor but Cost Nothing
081
人无远虑 必有近忧 People Who do not Think Far Ahead Will Inevitably Have Worries Near at Hand
089
其身正 不令而行 If the Ruler is Personally Upright, All Will Go Well Even Without His Orders
098
听其言而观其行 Listen to What One Says and Watch What He Does
106
后生可畏 The Younger Generation Will Surpass the Older
116
子见南子 Confucius Meeting with Nanzi
125
道不同不相为谋 No Common Goal, No Planning Together
134
四海之内皆兄弟 All Men are Brothers Wherever They Come from
141
在陈绝粮 Running out of Food When in Chen
150
子畏于匡 Confucius was Besieged in Kuang
158
子帅已正 孰敢不正 If the Ruler is Upright Himself, Who Dare not Be?
165
学而不厌 诲人不倦 Be Insatiable in Learning and Tireless in Teaching

目录 /comtents

有教无类

Educate All People Without Discrimination

子曰：" 有教无类。"——《卫灵公》
Confucius said, Educate all people without discrimination.——Wei Linggong

译：孔子说，"教学生不要分类别。"

子曰："自行束修以上，吾未尝无诲焉。"——《述而》
Confucius said, Only boys up to 15 can be taught by me.——Shuer

译：孔子说，"凡十五岁以上，我没有不收教的。"

■ 子曰："有教无类。"
　　Confucius said, Educate all people without discrimination.

　　译：孔子说，"教学生不要分类别。"

■ 子曰："自行束修以上，吾未尝无诲焉。"
　　Confucius said, Only boys up to 15 can be taught by me.

　　译：孔子说，"凡十五岁以上，我没有不收教的。"

《论语》名句故事

见贤思齐

**Try to Emulate Him
When You See a Good Man**

子曰:"见贤思齐焉,见不贤而内自省也。"——《里仁》

Confucius said, When you see a good man try to emulate him, when you see a bad man search yourself for his fault.——Liren

译:孔子说,"看到好人,便想如何向他看齐;看到不好的人,便反省自己。"

子曰:"今之孝者,是谓能养。至于犬马,皆能有养。不敬,何以别乎?"
——《为政》

Confucius said, What we call filial piety today means supporting one's parents. Peple also feed animals such as dogs and horses. Without respect, what's the difference? ——Weizheng

译:孔子说,"今天所谓的孝只讲能够养活父母。人也一样养活狗、马。不尊敬,那有什么区别?"

这个郯子是个了不起的人物啊！不但集德、才、威、雅于一身，还是一个至孝贤人呢。
Tanzi is really something. Not only a person with virtue, talent, power and elegance. But also a good person with filial piety.

据说原来郯子家很穷，可父母却是省吃俭用供他读书。并从言行举止上严格要求他，使他成了一个既有学问又有良好秉性修养的青年。
Tanzi's family used to be poor. His parents had to stint themselves of necessities for his education. Being strict with his words and behavior, he became a young man both learned and with kind nature and cultivation.

在他26岁那年，他父母双双得了眼疾，不久都双目失明了。为了给父母治病，他四处求医采药，几年下来父母的病没治好，家里的药渣都堆起了小山。
At the age of 26, his parents were both blind, suffering from eye illness. In order to cure their disease, he gathered herbs everywhere. After several yeas, his parents didn't recover even though medical slag has been piled up at home.

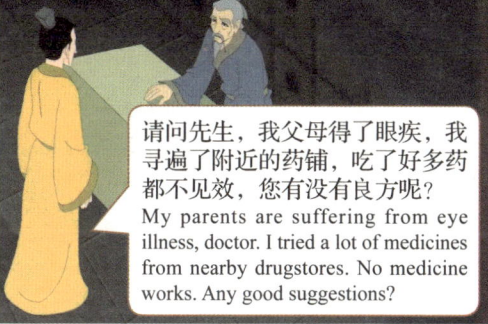

请问先生，我父母得了眼疾，我寻遍了附近的药铺，吃了好多药都不见效，您有没有良方呢？
My parents are suffering from eye illness, doctor. I tried a lot of medicines from nearby drugstores. No medicine works. Any good suggestions?

我世代行医，有一个方子治眼疾有奇效，可到我是第三代了，却没有人成功使用过。
We have practiced medicine for many years, one prescription works wonders. To me, it's the third generation, but no one has ever used it successfully.

太好了！请您开方取药，我来试试！
Great! Write out the prescription and let me try it please.

药好取，药引难求啊！要不然怎么三代了没有成功的病例呢？
Medicine is easy to get but guidingdrug is not. Otherwise why aren't there any successful cases until the third generation?

药引，是什么药引？！
Guidingdrug? What's it?

野鹿奶。
Milk of wild deer.

这个容易，森林和草原野鹿多得是，找到母鹿挤些就是了。
It's easy. There are a lot of wild deer in the forest and grassland. Find them and milk some.

呵呵，年轻人，取野鹿乳不是你想象的那么容易。每一个鹿群都有好几个公鹿负责警戒，一有风吹草动，鹿群就会跑得无影无踪。再者，你就是接近了鹿群也不能惊动母鹿，因为受到惊吓后的鹿乳其药用价值就会大大降低的。
Young man, it's not so easy as you think to get the milk. Every herd of deer has several male deer to be put on alert. The deer was soon out of sight at the mere rustle of leaves in the wind. What's more, even though you get close to the herd of deer, you cannot startle the female deer. Medical effect of the milk from a startled female deer will reduce greatly.

哦，原来是这样。
Oh, That is how it is.

怎样才能？
How can I ?

怎样才能够接近鹿群而不让它们受到惊吓呢？
How can I get close to the herd but not startle them?

郯子来到森林。
Tanzi came to the forest.

我要到森林里找到鹿群，见机行事。
I'll go to the forest, find the herd of deer and act according to the circumstance.

为了我们这几年你吃了不少苦啊，也老了许多。
You suffered a lot for us these years and older too.

娘，你千万不要这么说。为了父亲、母亲，儿吃再多的苦心里也是甜的，这些都是儿子应该做的啊！
Mother, never say that. For father, mother, I feel happy in heart even suffering more.These are all what a son should do for his parents.

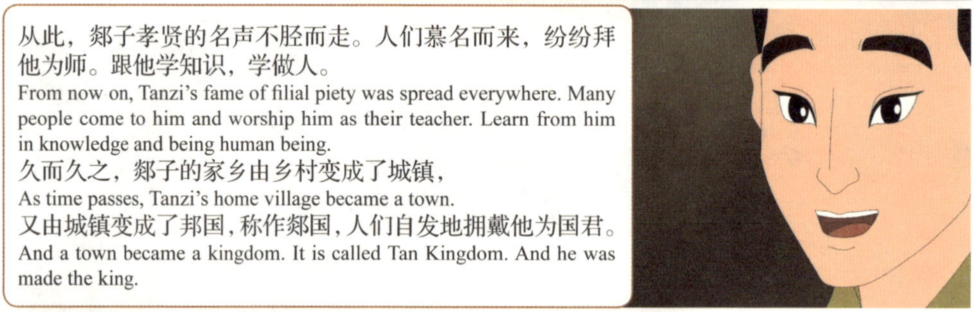

从此，郯子孝贤的名声不胫而走。人们慕名而来，纷纷拜他为师。跟他学知识，学做人。
From now on, Tanzi's fame of filial piety was spread everywhere. Many people come to him and worship him as their teacher. Learn from him in knowledge and being human being.
久而久之，郯子的家乡由乡村变成了城镇，
As time passes, Tanzi's home village became a town.
又由城镇变成了邦国，称作郯国，人们自发地拥戴他为国君。
And a town became a kingdom. It is called Tan Kingdom. And he was made the king.

当今人们讲孝，只能够养活父母。人也一样养活狗、牛等牲畜，不尊敬那有什么区别？贤哉！郯子！
what we call filial piety today means supporting one's parents. Peple also feed animals such as dogs and horses, without respect, what's the difference?

■ 子曰："今之孝者，是谓能养。至于犬马，皆能有养。不敬，何以别乎？"
Confucius said, What we call filial piety today means supporting one's parents. Peple also feed animals such as dogs and horses. Without respect, what's the difference?

译：孔子说，"今天所谓的孝只讲能够养活父母。人也一样养活狗、马。不尊敬，那有什么区别？"

> 夫子说的极是，我们走吧。
> Maser is right. Let's go.

■ 子曰："见贤思齐焉，见不贤而内自省也。"
Confucius said, When you see a good man try to emulate him, when you see a bad man search yourself for his fault.

译：孔子说，"看到好人，便想如何向他看齐；看到不好的人，便反省自己。"

人而无信 不知其可

If a Man Does not Keep His Word, What is He Good for？

子曰："人而无信，不知其可也。大车无輗，小车无軏，其何以行之哉？"
——《为政》

Confucius said, If a man does not keep his word, what is he good for? Can a carriage or cart drive without the crossbar?——Weizheng

译：孔子说，"人不守信任？那怎么可以？大车小车没有车轴，怎能行走？"

曾子曰："吾日三省吾身：为人谋而不忠乎？与朋友交而不信乎？传不习乎？"——《学而》

Zengzi said, I examine myself over and over every day: Whether I tried my best to do things for others, whether I kept my word when I get along with friends, Whether I reviewed what the teacher taught.——Xueer

译：曾子说，"我每天多次反省自己。为别人谋划考虑尽了心没有？交朋友，有没有不信实的地方？所传授给别人的东西，自己实践、研究过吗？"

你太小，那是大人去的地方。
You're too young. It's a place that only adults can go.

不，我都是大人了，我要去，要去嘛！
No. I'm older now. I want to go, go.

路很远，你走不到。就是你走到了，也走不回来的。
It's very far. You can not walk there. Even though you can be there, you can not walk home.
再说，母亲赶集有重要的事情要做，你去会误母亲的大事的。
What's more, mum has important thing to do. It'll be delayed with you.

我不嫌累，我也不误你的事。我要去，要去！
I won't be tired. I'll not delay you. I want to go, go.

曾元，曾元听话，父亲教你写字，在家等母亲。
Zengyuan, be good. Father will teach you write and let's wait for mother at home.

不！我不写字，我要去赶集！
No, I won't write. I'll go to the market.

嗯。
En.

你不整天吵着要肉吃吗？
Aren't you clamouring for meat all the time?

是啊。
Yes.

你出去时说，赶集回来给我杀猪吃肉的。
You said you'll kill the pig and let me have meat when you went for market.

刚才我是说过要杀猪的，那是骗曾元不让他跟我去赶集，你一个大人怎么能当真呢？
I said it a moment ago in order to cheat Zengyuan out of going market with me. How can you take it seriously as an adult?

我每天多次反省自己，为别人办事情尽心了没有？跟朋友交往讲究信用了没有？老师传授的知识温习了没有？
I examine myself over and over every day. Whether I tried my best to do things for others, whether I kept my word when I get along with friends and whether I reviewed what the teacher taught.
做人啊要不断地反省自己，反省自己说过的话，做过的事。
As a human being, we should examine ourselves frequently about what we said and what we did.

■ 曾子曰："吾日三省吾身：为人谋而不忠乎？与朋友交而不信乎？传不习乎？"
Zengzi said, I examine myself over and over every day: Whether I tried my best to do things for others, whether I kept my word when I get along with friends , Whether I reviewed what the teacher taught.

译：曾子说，"我每天多次反省自己。为别人谋划考虑尽了心没有？交朋友，有没有不信实的地方？所传授给别人的东西，自己实践、研究过吗？"

行了，行了，我赞成你修身做人的这套道理，可这与杀猪有什么关系呢？
Ok, ok. I agree to your rules of cultivation and behavior. But what does that got to with killing the pig?

怎能说没关系呢？
How can you say not?
孔夫子教诲说：一个人要是不讲信用，就不知道他能成就什么事情了。
Confucius taught us, if someone doesn't keep his word. What is he good for?
信用就像大车的輗、小车的軏，没有了就无法行走。
Credit is like the crossbar of carriage and cart. No carriage or cart can drive with it.

人活在世上，为人处世要讲诚信，对小孩子更是不能哄骗的。
Living in the world, we should keep our word and don't cheat kids.
比如说今天的事情，你做母亲的，怎么可以欺骗孩子呢？
Take the case of today as an example, as a mother, how can you cheat your son?
父母是孩子最最信赖的人，同时也是孩子的第一任老师，你今天欺骗了他，是教他学习欺骗。
Parents are the persons that kids trust most and at the same time the first teachers of them. If you cheat him today, you'll teach him cheating others.

他以父母为榜样，按照父母的教导和样子去做事的。
He'll follow his parents' instructions and models to do things.
等他长大成人，也学着你的样子去欺骗你，欺骗别人，那怎么得了？
After he grow up, he'll learn from you and cheat you. Cheat others, that's serious.

■ 子曰："人而无信，不知其可也。大车无輗，小车无軏，其何以行之哉？"

Confucius said, If a man does not keep his word, what is he good for? Can a carriage or cart drive without the crossbar?

译：孔子说，"人不守信任？那怎么可以？大车小车没有车轴，怎能行走？"

温故而知新
Gain New Knowledge by Reviewing Old

子曰:"温故而知新,可以为师矣。"——《为政》
Confucius said, To learn new by reviwing the old. That's a way of study. ——Weizheng

译:孔子说,"温习过去,已知道未来,这样便可以做老师了。"

听了夫子的宏论，让我茅塞顿开。原来音乐也能表达人生的重点命题呀。听君一席话，胜读十年书啊！
Your splendid theory enlightens me immediately. Music can express the key subject of human life. Your words are worthy of ten years of reading.

我再演奏一曲。
I'll play one piece again.

这支曲子……
This piece of music…

夫子莫讲，这支曲子的意境太深邃了。
Don't speak, the artistic conception of this piece of music is too profound.

容丘记下乐谱，练习几天，自己体会，再行请教好吗？
Let me record the music and practice for a few days. First experience it myself and then ask you for advice, ok?

行，太好了！有思想！
All right. Great! Good idea.

那，夫子告辞了。
Good bye, master.

好，请慢走。
Ok, see you.

三天后
Three days later

好！好！
All right.

夫子，我把曲子演奏一遍，容您指教。
Master, let me play the music for your instruction.

美轮美奂！绝妙无比！
Great! Marvelous!
先生已经体会到了这支曲子意境的深邃。
You have already understood the true artistic conception of the music.

当我熟悉了曲谱和弹奏方法后，边弹边体会。
After I was familiar with its music and way of play, I tried to understand it with my heart while playing.

我感觉有个古人站在我的面前，他皮肤微黑，身材高大，他庄重威严而又和善可亲，浑身上下散发着一股天子之气，我想这不就是供奉在庙里的周文王吗？
I feel that an ancient person standing in front of me. With dark skin and tall figure, he is solemn but amiable, perfectly look like a king. Isn't he King Zhouwen enshrined in the temple?

对，对呀！这支曲子就是《文王操》。
Right, right. This piece of music is about him.

几天功夫就深得周乐之精义，先生真是圣人啊！
Fully understand the gist of Zhou music. You're really a saint, sir.

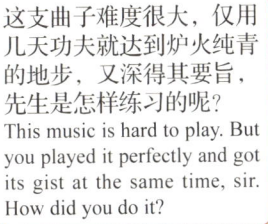

■ 子曰："温故而知新，可以为师矣。"
Confucius said, To learn new by reviwing the old. That's a way of study.

译：孔子说，"温习过去，已知道未来，这样便可以做老师了。"

钓而不钢 弋不射宿

Fish Without a Fishnet and Hunt Without Shooting at Animals that are Sleeping

厩焚。子退朝，曰："伤人乎？"不问马。——《乡党》
The barn was burnt. Confucius came back from the court and asked, "Does anyone got hurt?" He didn't ask about the horses. ——Xiangdang

译：马厩失火。孔子从朝廷回来后说，"伤人了吗？"没有问马。

子钓而不钢，弋不射宿。——《述而》
Confucius fishes without a fishnet and hunts without shooting at animals that are sleeping. ——Shuer

译：孔子钓鱼，但不用绳网捕鱼。孔子射鸟，但不射栖宿巢中的鸟。

失火啦！失火啦！快来救火啊！
Fire! On fire! Come to put it out quickly!

啊！
Oh.

快来救火啊！
Come to put the fire out quickly!

失火啦！失火啦！快来救火啊！
Fire! On fire! Come to put it out quickly!

快来救火啊！
Come to put the fire out quickly!

《论语》名句故事

啊!
Oh!

不好!难道是我家失火啦?
Oh, no. is my house on fire?

42

啊!
Oh!

怎么回事，哪里失火啦?
What's up? Where is the fire?

是马厩，对不起夫子，是我不小心燃着了粮草引起了大火。
It's the barn. Sorry, master. It's my carelessness that caused this fire.

好在扑救及时，没有殃及其它房屋。
It's nice that we put it out in time. Other houses are saved.

伤人了没有？
Does anyone get hurt?

没有伤人。
No.

谢天谢地，没伤人就好，没伤人就好！
Thank god. It's ok that nobody was hurt. Fine.

马厩失火是我的过错，您没有一声埋怨，而知道没有伤人您就满意了。老夫实在感动！
It's my fault that the barn is on fire. You don't blame me. You're happy that nobody was hurt. I'm really moved.

夫子的仁爱之心如日月的光辉，永照人间。
Your benevolence is like light of the sun and the moon, shine the world forever.

你也不要太自责，以后小心就是了。
Don't blame yourself too much. Be carful from now on.

■ 厩焚。子退朝，曰："伤人乎？"不问马。
The barn was burnt. Confucius came back from the court and asked, "Does anyone got hurt?" He didn't ask about the horses.

译：马厩失火。孔子从朝廷回来后说，"伤人了吗？"没有问马。

子路，子路。
Zilu, Zilu.

夫子，子路在。有何吩咐？
Master, Zilu's here. Anything I can do for you?

今天朝中无事，你收拾工具，我们到沂河钓鱼。
I have nothing to do at court. Pack up tools, let's go fishing in River Yi.

钓鱼？是！
Fishing? Yes, master.

嗯。
Ok.

呵呵。
Hehe (Laughter).

呵呵。
Hehe (Laughter).

很久没有出来打猎，手都有些生疏了。
Haven't gone hunting for a long time, I am out of practice.

嘿，不亏是行家里手，收获颇丰啊！
Hey. You're really a master. Heavy gain.

您钓的鱼也一定很多吧？
You must fish a lot.

啊？只有两条啊！
Ah, only two?

这点比你差远了。
I'm worse compared with you.

夫子，何必这么麻烦，我已给您准备了鱼网，一网下去比您钓一天要多好几倍。
Master, Why do you trouble yourself so much? I prepare a fishnet for you. You'll get several times of what you fish a day by casting the net once.

住手！何必要赶尽杀绝呢？
Stop! Is there any need to kill them off?

鱼是逮不尽的。
Fishes can not be caught off.

钓而不纲弋不射宿
Fish Without a Fishnet and Hunt Without Shooting at Animals that are Sleeping

我钓鱼只是享受这个过程和乐趣。
When fishing, I'm enjoying the process and fun of it.

你是一网下去，大鱼小鱼尽收网底。
While casting the net once, all fishes either big or small are all caught.

大鱼且不说，那小鱼刚刚出生，还没享受到生命的乐趣，岂不可惜！你是猎人出身，我不反对你打猎。
That's ok for big ones. But small ones were born a short time ago. They haven't experienced the fun of life. What a pity! You were born from a hunting family. I don't object you hunting.

但是，无论鸟类还是各种动物，在它们睡觉的时候是不允许打的。
But whether birds or other kinds of animals, you are not allowed to shoot at them.

知道是为什么吗？
Do you know why?

夫子仁慈博爱之心可见。
It's obviously out of master's benevolence.

■ **子钓而不纲，弋不射宿。**
Confucius fishes without a fishnet and hunts without shooting at animals that are sleeping.

译：孔子钓鱼，但不用绳网捕鱼。孔子射鸟，但不射栖宿巢中的鸟。

《论语》名句故事

节用而爱人
Be Economical and Love People

子曰:"道千乘之国,敬事而信,节用而爱人,使民以时。"——《学而》
To govern a country with more than 1,000 chariots, dedicate yourself to work and be faithful, be economical and love people. Use them in proper time. ——Xueer

译:孔子说,"治理有千辆兵车的国家,慎重、敬畏地处理政事,恪守信任,节省开支,爱护人民,差使老百姓选择农闲的时候。"

子曰:"小子识之,苛政猛于虎也!"——《檀弓》
Keep in mind, boys! A bad government is more fearful than a tiger. —— Tangong

译:孔子说,"弟子们记住,严酷繁重的赋税比老虎还要凶猛可怕!"

节用而爱人 *Be Economical and Love People*

听，这女人哭的好伤心那。
Listen to this woman cries well sad that.

我年青时当过吹鼓手，常给人家办丧事，从这妇人的哭声，我能听出亡者是她的儿子，我们去劝慰一下吧！
I used to be a trumpeter and help with other's funerals. This woman's cry tells me that the dead is her son. Let's go and comfort her.

人死不能复生，小心哭坏了身体，你这么悲痛，哭的是何人那？
Be careful with your health. You know one can not come back to life. You're so sad, whom are you crying for?

是我的儿子新亡。
My son died.

哦！这儿座坟又埋的何人？
Oh. Whose tombs are these?

51

《论语》名句故事

是我的公公和我的男人。
My father-in-law and my husband's.

太让人痛心了，他们都是因何而死？
Too painful! How did they die?

我们一家三代 住在这深山野岭，以打猎为生。
Our three generations are living deep into the mountains and make a living on hunting.

前些年，公公因狩猎被老虎吃掉了，最后只找到几块骨头，埋在这里。
My father was bitten by a tiger several years ago. Some bones of him were found and buried here.

昨天，我还不到十岁的儿子又被老虎叼走了，连块骨头也没找到，这里边埋的是他生前的几件破衣服。
Yesterday, my son, not up to 10, was got away by a tiger. Nothing was found What I buried here is clothes that he wore.

两年前，我男人又被老虎咬死，埋在了这里。
Two years ago, my husband was bitten by a tiger and died also. I buried him here.

52

你明明知道山中有虎，你的公公和男人又先后被虎吃掉，为什么不早点搬到山下去住？
You know clearly that there're tigers in mountains. And your father and husband were bitten by tigers one after the other. Why didn't you move away from the mountains?

如果搬离这里，你儿子也不会惨遭不幸了！
If you moved away, your son wouldn't be dead.

唉！我何尝没想过这个问题啊！可在山下更难那！
Oh. I also think about this. But it's more difficult down the mountain.

在山下住更难？这话从何谈起？
It's more difficult? Why?

你们是过路人，有所不知。
You're passers-by and don't know.

我们原先也住在山下的村子里，靠种田为生，可在山下住，官府的苛捐杂税多如牛毛，一旦交不上，官府的人不是打就是抓，实在活不下去了，才搬到这深山野外。
We used to live in the village and live on farming. But living there, we had to pay many taxes. If not, guards would either beat or catch you. It's hard to live. So we moved into the wild mountains.

这里虽然有虎，却没有贪官，没有那么多的苛捐杂税。
Even there're tigers here, no greedy officers, no taxes.

弟子们那，你们要牢牢地记住，苛政比凶猛的老虎害人还厉害呀！
Students, keep this in mind, A bad government is more fearful than a tiger.

《论语》名句故事

一处有虎不能把这里的人都吃掉，可一处有暴政却无一人能幸免。
Tigers in one place cannot eat out all people here. But a bad government will do harm to everyone.

我们记下了！
Got it, master.

夫子，怎样才能治理好一个国家，让百姓安居乐业呢？
Master, how can we rule a country well, and let people living a happy life?

你们将来有机会出仕为官，比如说要治理一个拥有上千辆兵车的国家，
If you have chance to be officers, e.g. to govern a country with more than 1,000 chariots .
一是要敬业，不能敷衍行事；二是要诚信，不能欺人；三是要节俭，不能奢侈，以减轻百姓负担；四是爱人，以人为本；最后就是，即使要役使百姓、征收赋税，也要适时而行。
First, dedicate yourself to work, don't skip anything;
Secondly, be faithful and conceive nobody;
Thirdly, practice thrift and don't be luxurious so as to ease the burden of people.
Fourthly, love people and take people as the most important .
The last is, Even if you have to use people and lay tax on them, you should do it in proper time.

■ 子曰:"小子识之,苛政猛于虎也!"
Keep in mind, boys! A bad government is more fearful than a tiger.

译: 孔子说,"弟子们记住,严酷繁重的赋税比老虎还要凶猛可怕!"

■ 子曰:"道千乘之国,敬事而信,节用而爱人,使民以时。"
To govern a country with more than 1,000 chariots, dedicate yourself to work and be faithful, be economical and love people, Use them in proper time.

译: 孔子说,"治理有千辆兵车的国家,慎重、敬畏地处理政事,恪守信任,节省开支,爱护人民,差使老百姓选择农闲的时候。"

弟子牢记夫子教诲。
Keep what master said in mind.

我们一定牢记夫子教诲,敬事而信,节用而爱人。
We'll surely keep what master said in mind, dedicated ourselves to work, be economical and love people.

是。
Yes, master.

拿些钱和干粮,让这位夫人下山安个家过日子吧。
Give this woman some money and solid food, let her leave here and make home in a village.

谢谢恩人,谢谢恩人!
Thank you, benefactor. Thank you.

不必客气,快快请起!
My pleasure. Stand up quickly.

我们赶快上路吧!
Let's move on quickly.

是。
Yes.

父母在 不远游

Don't Travel far from Home if Parents are still Living

子曰:"父母在,不远游,游必有方。"——《里仁》

Confucius said, Don't travel far from home if parents are still living. If have to, a destination must be told. ——Liren

译:孔子说,"父母活着的时候,不远走高飞。如果走,也要有一定的方向。"

子曰:"子生三年,然后免于父母之怀。夫三年之丧,天下之通丧也。"
——《阳货》

Confucius said, Sons don't leave their parents' arms until they are three years old. So it is a common rule that one should observe mourning for one's parent for three years. —— Yanghuo

译:孔子说,"儿女生下三年后才脱离父母亲的怀抱。这个三年的丧制,是大家都遵行的一般规则。"

唉！看来我跟晏婴只能做朋友，道不同不相为谋。
Oh. It seems that Yanying and I can only be friends. We can not cooperate with each other with different ideas.

晏婴啊，不相为谋啊！
Yanying, can not cooperate.

啊？难道……
Ah, didn't he…?

好了，好了。
Well, forget it.

我们明天去齐国的边境小镇堂阜拜见昭公。
Let's leave for the border town of Qi to meet Zhaogong.

现在我们出去走走，顺便了解这里的风土人情。
Now, let's walk around here and know some local conditions and customs.

《论语》名句故事

夫子，你看！
Master, look!

这位先生，看你年纪轻轻，为什么要寻短见？
Sir, why do you commit suicide at such a young age?
有什么悲伤的事情非要走这条路呢？
What misery makes you do this?

我少年离家，四方求学，
I have travelled everywhere for study since my childhood.
想学成后谋得一官半职，奉养父母的养育之恩。
I wanted to pay back my parents for all their support after I finished my study and got a position.

可谁曾想，学问学到了，官没谋到，
Who knows I'm learned now, but no position was offered.
回到家后父母早已双亡。
My parents both died when I was back home.
我还有什么颜面活在这个世上啊！呜呜……
How can I live in this world? (Sob.)

父母在不远游 Don't Traveled far from Home if Parents are still Living

赶快救人！快！
Hurry, Help!

太可惜了，那人死得太可惜了！
What a pity! What a pity the man died.

是啊，是太可惜了！这件事对我触动也很大。
It's really a pity. It moved me deeply.
我带你们出来也犯了个错误。
I made a mistake to let you travel with me.

啊！犯了错误？
Ah. A mistake.

是啊，你们家中要是有父母需要照顾的话，赶快回家；
Yes Go home quickly if you have parents to take care of.

如果不需要照顾，可随我远游，
If not, travel with me.
但也要经常给父母捎回家书，说明你所在的地方。
But write to parents often and let them know where you are.

■ 子曰："父母在，不远游，游必有方。"
Confucius said, Don't travel far from home if parents are still living. If have to, a destination must be told.

译：孔子说，"父母活着的时候，不远走高飞。如果走，也要有一定的方向。"

先生，我父亲有病在身，我要回去侍俸他。
Master, my father is ill. I have to go back to take care of him.

夫子，我父母都年纪大了，身边没人不行。
Master, my parents are both old, they cannot do without me.

我也要回家。
I want to go home.

好，好。我们出来的匆忙，这个事情是我考虑不周。
Well, It was very thoughtless of me. We come out in a hurry.
明天你们就可以收拾行囊回家。
Pack up and go home tomorrow.
记住，父母在时要精心奉养，父母不在了要守三年的丧。
Remember: Take good care of them when your parents are living. Observe mourning for your parents for three years when they are dead.

夫子，居丧守孝三年，时间太久了吧！
Master, it's too long to observe mourning for three years!

君子三年不参加礼仪活动，礼一定会生疏，
If one doesn't attend any ceremony for three years, he will be out of practice.
三年不练习音乐就会忘记。
If one doesn't practice music, he will forget.

陈粮吃尽，新谷登场，我看一年就可以了。
New cereal will appear if the old grain was eaten out. In my view, one year is enough.

父母去世了，吃好粮食，穿好衣服，你安心吗？
Parents died, can you feel at ease to have good food and fine clothes?

安心！
Yes, I can.

你安心？你就那样做好了！
Do as you like if that's the case.

君子守孝时，应当是吃饭没有味道，听音乐也不感到快乐，早晚起居也不安心。你说你安心，你去做吧！去！去！
When observing mourning for their parents, one should have not much taste for food. Don't feel happy when listening to music. Don't feel at ease in their daily life. You can be at ease. Go and do what you like. Go.

师弟，师弟。
Young brother, young brother.
宰我！
Zaiwo!

父母在不远游
Don't Traveled far from Home if Parents are still Living

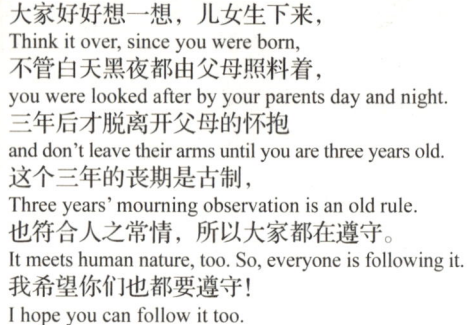

让他走吧！宰我真是没有仁爱之心啊！
Let him go. Zaiwo has no heart of benevolence.

大家好好想一想，儿女生下来，
Think it over, since you were born,
不管白天黑夜都由父母照料着，
you were looked after by your parents day and night.
三年后才脱离开父母的怀抱
and don't leave their arms until you are three years old.
这个三年的丧期是古制，
Three years' mourning observation is an old rule.
也符合人之常情，所以大家都在遵守。
It meets human nature, too. So, everyone is following it.
我希望你们也都要遵守！
I hope you can follow it too.

我真搞不明白，难道那宰我没有得到父母三年的关爱吗？
I really don't know Zaiwo. Didn't he have his parents' three years of care?

■ 子曰："子生三年 然后免于父母之怀。夫三年之丧，天下之通丧也。"

Confucius said, Sons don't leave their parents' arms until they are three years old. So it is a common rule that one should observe mourning for one's parent for three years.

译：孔子说，"儿女生下三年后才脱离父母亲的怀抱。这个三年的丧制，是大家都遵行的一般规则。"

知之为知之

Knowing is Knowing

子曰:"知之为知之,不知为不知,是知也。"——《为政》
Confucius said, Knowing is knowing, not knowing is not, which is really wise.
——Wei Zheng

译:孔子说,"知道就是知道,不知道就是不知道,这就是真正的'智慧'。"

《论语》名句故事

我说得对！我说得对！
I'm right. I'm right.

我对你不对！我对！
I'm right. You're wrong. I'm right.

嗯？
En?

哼！就是我对！哼！是我对你不对！我对你不对！
Hum. It's me who are right. Hum. I'm right. You're wrong. I'm right, you're wrong.

哼！就是我对！哼！我对你不对！我对你不对！
Hum. It's me who are right. Hum. I'm right. You're wrong. I'm right, you're wrong.

噢？你是谁呀？
Oh, who are you?

二位童子，你们在争论什么？连路也顾不得让。
Kids, what are you arguing? You're in our way.

我是鲁国的孔丘。
I'm Kong Qiu from Kingdom Lu

孔丘？你就是无书不读的孔圣人？
Kong Qiu, you are the well-read saint?

啊？你就是无书不读的孔圣人？
Ah, you are the well-read saint?
是啊，我是孔丘却不是什么圣人。
Yes, I'm Kong Qiu but not a so called saint.
你来得正巧，给我们评一评理到底谁说得对。
You're just the person. Please judge for us who is the right.
谁说得对？谁说得对？
Who is right？ who is right？
哈哈哈……
Ha ha ha…
滚！小孩子有什么是非。
Get out of here. Kids have no right or wrong.
夫子不要理他们，我们继续赶路吧。
Master, don't mind them let's move forward.
休得无理，或许他们争论的是一个很有意思的问题呢？也或许对我们有启发呢？
Don't be rude, what they debate may be an interesting question. Perhaps it's instructive to us.
二位童子说说看，你们争论的是什么问题啊？
Kids, tell me what's the problem you're debating.

我先说，太阳……
Me first, the sun...

我先说，太阳……
Me first, the sun...

哈哈哈……
Ha ha ha...

好好好，一个一个的说，我都仔细听。
Ok, ok, tell me one by one, I promise listen to you carefully.

你先说吧，你们争论的是什么问题？
You first, what's the problem?

我们争论的是太阳何时离地面最近
When is the sun nearest to the earth?

小小年纪竟然争论连大人都想不到的问题，可见楚国的教化不同凡响啊！
Kids of your age are debating a problem that even adults seldom think of. How extraordinary the education of Kingdom Chu is!

依你之见，太阳何时离地面最近呢？
In your view, when is the sun nearest to the earth?

早晨和下午太阳离地面最近。
In the morning, and in the afternoon.

有何道理呢?
Why?

日出东方和日薄西山时,太阳大如车轮。
In sunrise and sunset, the sun is as big as a wheel.

而日近中午时却小如圆盘,凡人视物近者大而远者小。
But when near noon, the sun is as small as a plate. It's a common sense that something looks bigger when it's near, while looks smaller when it's far.

所以嘛,我说早和晚太阳离地面最近。
So I say the sun is nearest to the earth in the morning and in the late afternoon.

好!言之有理,言之有理啊!
Good, it makes sense. It makes sense.

不对,不对!他说得不对!
Wrong, wrong, what he said is wrong.

不对,不对!她说得不对!
Wrong, wrong, what she said is wrong.

《论语》名句故事

不要吵，不要吵，那你说说看，
Don't quarrel, don't quarrel. Well, you say.

早与晚的太阳凉嗖嗖的，而中午的太阳灼热如火酷热难奈，凡人感物，近者热而远者凉。
The sun is cool in the morning and in the late afternoon. But at noon, it's as hot as fire and too hard for people. It's also a common sense that something is hot when it's near, while it's cool when far.

所以嘛，我说中午的太阳离地面最近。
So I say the sun is nearest to the earth at noon.

嗯，言之凿凿，言之凿凿啊！
En, reasonable, reasonable.

一个是"言之有理"，一个是"言之凿凿"，到底谁说得对啊？
One is makes sense, the other is reasonable. Who on earth is right?

嗯……这……
En...this...

哼！
Hum.

我们谁说得对啊？快回答！
Who is right? Quickly.

二位童子，实在对不起，你们的问题我也弄不明白。
Kids, I'm so sorry. I have no idea on your question.

这，这……
This, this…

嗯？
En?

都说你是无书不读的圣人，我才不信呢！
You're said to be a well-read saint, I can't believe.

唉，看来圣人也不比别人知道得多啊！
A saint knows no more than the others.

咱们走吧，走吧。
Let's go, go.

《论语》名句故事

夫子，夫子。
Master, master.

夫子，你何必那么认真呢？你就说他们其中一个说得对就是了，也免得受那孩童欺辱！
Master, why are you so serious? Just say either of them is right. The kids wouldn't tease at you.

就是，就是。
That's it, that's it.

嗯，休得胡言！人在世上要童叟无欺，更何况他们的问题我就是不懂。
En. Stop nonsense! We should cheat nobody either kids or the elders. What's more, I really don't know the answer to their question.

对任何问题，不懂就不要装懂，知道的就是知道，不知道的就是不知道，这才是智慧啊！
Whatever the problem, we mustn't pretend to understand if we don't. Knowing is knowing, not knowing is not, which is really wise.

■ 子曰："知之为知之，不知为不知，是知也。"
Confucius said, Knowing is knowing, not knowing is not, which is really wise.

译：孔子说，"知道就是知道，不知道就是不知道，这就是真正的'智慧'。"

夫子，为什么这么说啊？
Master, why do you say so?

道理很简单，一方面说明你是一个诚实的人，另一方面，把你知道的传授给别人，不也是一件很快乐的事情吗？
The point is simple, on the one hand, it shows that you're honest. On the other, teach others what you know, isn't it pleasant?

你不知道的去认真学习，努力探索不是丰富了你的才能和智慧吗？
Study carefully what you don't know, isn't it enrich your skill and intelligence by studying hard?

是，是。
Yes, yes.

惠而不费
Doing Favor but Cost Nothing

子贡曰:"贫而无谄,富而无骄,何如?"子曰:"可也。未若贫而乐,富而好礼者也。"——《学而》

Zigong said, To be poor and yet not to be servile; to be rich and yet not to be proud, what do you say to that? It is good, replied Confucius, but better still it is to be poor and yet contented; to be rich and yet know how to be courteous.

——Xueer

译:子贡说:"贫穷而不逢迎谄媚,富裕而不骄矜傲慢,怎么样?"孔子说,"好。但不如贫穷但快乐,虽富裕却爱好礼制。"

子曰:"因民之所利而利之,斯不亦惠而不费乎?"——《尧曰》

Confucius answered, Do people favor for their benefits, isn't it doing favor but costing nothing? ——Yaoyue

译:孔子说,"根据民众利益而去做,这不就是施恩惠而不花费吗?"

大家快来看今天有肉吃喽!
Come and look, everyone. We'll have meat to eat today.

有肉吃啦!
Meat to eat?
这是怎么回事?
What's up?

子路,你这是哪里弄的牛?
Zilu, where do you get the cattle from?

我这是……
It's…

好！很好！杀牛吃肉，今天改善伙食。
Very good. Kill the cattle and let's have a better meal today.

太好啦！这要感谢子路兄啊！
Great! Thanks to Brother Zilu.

哼！做了好事还要人家的报酬，算什么君子！夫子竟然还赞扬他？
Oh. Help others but accepting their reward. What good is he? Master praised him for this.

数月以后
A few months later

夫子经常在众人面前夸颜回安穷乐道。
Master often praises Yanhui for his being contented in poverty and devoted to things spiritual.
子路救人要人家的牛还得到了他的表扬。
Zilu saved someone's life but got a cattle as a reward. Master praised him, too.
这回我要让夫子好好夸奖我一番。
I'll let master praise me a lot this time.

我们的问题暂一放,你们师兄回来啦,看他这几个月在外面有什么见闻。
Let's just stop here on this subject. Your elder brother comes back. Let's see what he has experienced these months.

拜见夫子。
Good morning, Master.

也没有什么见闻,这趟生意还算顺手。
Nothing new. The business was done without a hitch
挣了钱我就在想一个问题。
I'm thinking over one problem after making money.

哦？想的什么问题？
Oh, what's it?

好！
Good.

我在想过去我贫穷的时候，在那些贵人和富人面前虽然心里有些不痛快，可是，我也不以为耻，更没向他们奉承谄媚。
I'm thinking when I was poor. Although I felt bad in the face of the noble and the rich I was shameless about it. Neither was I servile to them.

现在我经商富了，也没有对别人摆出漠视和傲慢的模样。夫子，您认为如何？
Now I'm rich. But I never gave a neglecting and arrogant look to others. Master, how do you think?

不过，不如虽贫穷却快乐，虽富裕却爱好礼制。
But not better than to be poor and yet contented; to be rich and yet know how to be courteous.

■ 子贡曰："贫而无谄，富而无骄，何如？"子曰："可也。未若贫而乐，富而好礼者也。"
Zigong said, To be poor and yet not to be servile; to be rich and yet not to be proud, what do you say to that? It is good, replied Confucius, but better still it is to be poor and yet contented; to be rich and yet know how to be courteous.

译：子贡说："贫穷而不逢迎谄媚，富裕而不骄矜傲慢，怎么样？"孔子说，"好。但不如贫穷但快乐，虽富裕却爱好礼制。"

这次我经商时，遇到了一个在国外沦为奴隶的鲁国人，我把他给赎了回来，交给了官府。
When I was doing business this time, I met a citizen of Lu who was reduced to slavery. I paid for his freedom and gave him to the authorities.

好！太好了！
Great! Great!

师兄做得对，这是有仁有义的大好事啊。
Well-done brother! It's great thing of benevolence.

是啊，鲁国的这个政策很好，也很人道。按规定你可以到国库中报销你付的赎金哪，你去了吗？
Yes. The policy of Lu is really good and humane. According to rule, you can get back what you paid from the authorities. Did you?

没有去领赎金，这点钱对我来说算不上什么。再说了，我这样做不是比那些赎回奴隶又到国库领取赎金的人更高尚吗？
No. this amount of money is nothing to me. What's more, What I did is more respectable than those who paid for the slavers, but get the money back from the government, isn't it?

子贡，我知道你有钱，但这件事，你做得不对！
Zigong, I know you are rich. But on this matter, You're wrong.

夫子，我怎么又不对啦？我总比那些救了人又要人家答谢的人好吧？我怎样做才是对的？
Master, why am I wrong again? Am I better than those who saved others but got a reward? What should I do?

夫子，我们还是继续讨论刚才的话题吧。
Master, shall we continue to discuss our topic?

好，继续刚才的话题。
All right. Let's go on with our topic.

子贡啊，你不要走，刚才的话题正好可以解答你的疑惑。
Zigong, don't go away. Our discussion can answer your question.

刚才您说到从政的五美，那么，什么叫施恩惠而不花费呢？
You said about the "five beauties" of political career. Then, what's doing favor but costing nothing?

根据民众的利益而去做，这不就是施恩惠而不花费吗？
Do people favor for their benefits, isn't it doing favor but costing nothing?

■ 子曰："因民之所利而利之，斯不亦惠而不费乎？"
Confucius answered, Do people favor for their benefits, isn't it doing favor but costing nothing?

译：孔子说，"根据民众利益而去做，这不就是施恩惠而不花费吗？"

我们就拿你们两位师兄的例子进一步解释这个问题吧。
Let's take your two brothers' stories as examples to explain it in detail.

子贡赎人而不去领赎金，这本来无可厚非。
Zigong's paying for the slaver without getting the money back. It's good.

可你让别人怎么办？去领吧，好像不如子贡道德高尚；不领，自己就得自掏腰包。
But what should others do? Go to get the money back, they are not as noble as Zigong. If not, they have to pay from their wallet.

长此以往，谁还愿意去做这样的事情？那么国家的条文不就成了一纸空文了吗？鲁国人不是继续在国外做奴隶吗？
As time goes on, who are willing to do this kind of thing? If that's the case, the policy of the country will be useless. And Lu's citizens will still be slavers abroad, won't they?

对，对，对！
Right, yes.
原来道理在这里呀！
That's it.

我们再说子路救人，人家感谢他，他收了人家一头牛。我说好，好在哪里？好在这样做会鼓励更多的人去做好事。
Let's get back to Zilu's story. He saved a boy and they are grateful. He accept a cattle as a reward. I said yes to him. Why? Because it makes more people do good deeds.

夫子，我错了。我知道我错在哪里了。
Master, it's my fault. And I know where my fault is.

知道就好。
That's enough.

人无远虑 必有近忧
People Who do not Think Far Ahead Will Inevitably Have Worries Near at Hand

子曰："人无远虑，必有近忧。"——《卫灵公》
Confucius said, People who do not think far ahead will inevitably have worries near at hand. ——Weilinggong

译：孔子说，"人没有长远的考虑，必然会有近在眼前的忧愁。"

子路使子羔为费宰。子曰："贼夫人之子。"子路曰："有民人焉，有社稷焉，何必读书，然为学？"子曰："是故恶夫佞者。"——《先进》
Zilu made Zigao governor of Fei. Confucius said, You did him harm. Zilu said, There are people need him to govern and imperial divine temple need him to worship. Isn't one learned by reading only? Confucius said, So I hate persons with bad excuses.
——Xianjin

译：子路要子羔做费地方的官长。孔子说，"害了人家孩子。"子路说，"有老百姓，有土地庄稼，何必一定读书，才算学问？"孔子说，"所以我讨厌狡辩的人。"

孔丘拜见国君。
Kongqiu worship your majesty.

夫子来了，快快请进。
Master's coming. Come in quickly.

今天就你我二人，不必行此大礼，我们随便坐。
There are only two of us. Don't kowtow and sit down please.

不知国君召孔丘有何要事？
What is the meeting for?

夫子啊，您入宫以来，我国国力渐强，特别是夹谷之会，您为我鲁国赢得了很大的荣誉，在各国中，鲁国又有了大国的气度，再不愁内忧外患了。
Master, our country is becoming strong and powerful since you came into office. Especially at Jiagu Meeting, you won great honor for Kingdom Lu. Lu is now becoming a great power among all kingdoms. And has no fear of internal disturbance and foreign aggression.

不，不！外患暂时可以说缓解了，只有我们国力真正强大了，才能享受真正的太平。
No. no. Foreign aggression is now easing, we can enjoy real peace only when we are powerful enough.

可内忧不但存在，我认为还很严重。
But internal disturbance is now still here, and even more serious.

哦，有什么内忧呢？
Oh, what's it?

三都！
Three cities.

您想把三都怎么样？
What are you going to do with the three cities?

拆除！
Destroy them.

不可，不可，那可是三桓的命根子呀！
No, no. That's the lifeblood of three prime ministers.

按照周礼，大臣不能收藏武器，上卿大夫不能拥有长三百丈，高一丈的城墙。
Ministers cannot store weapons according to Zhouli. Prime minister can not have city wall of 300 zhang long and 1 zhang high.
而我国三家上卿大夫的食邑之城都远超过了这个标准。
But the cities of our three prime ministers all surpass this standard.

要想抵御外侵，富民强国，长治久安必须抑私家，强公室。
We have to strengthen royal family by controlling others if we want to defend our country from foreign invasion and become powerful.

他们三家的势力强大，我怕他们不肯，引起内乱呀！
Three of them are all powerful. I'm afraid it will cause internal disturbance if they are not willing to.

国君啊，无论是国家和一个家庭，或者是个人，没有长远的考虑，必然会有近在眼前的忧患。
King, whether for a country, family or person, if it do not think far ahead, they will inevitably have worries near at hand.

■ 子曰："人无远虑，必有近忧。"
Confucius said, People who do not think far ahead will inevitably have worries near at hand.

译：孔子说，"人没有长远的考虑，必然会有近在眼前的忧愁。"

当年昭公屈辱的去齐，现在季桓子的养虎为患就是很好的例子。
Zhaogong went to Qi with humiliation that year. Now, Ji Huanzi, a warmed snake in bosom are two good lessons.

夫子言之有理，可……可怎么才能让季桓子堕毁他的费邑，孟懿子堕毁他的咸城，叔孙氏坠毁他的郈城呢？
Master is right. But how can we let Ji Huanzi destroy his City Fei? Meng Yizi destroy his City Xian and Shu Sunshi destroy his City Hou?

这个不难，您只要当着文武百官提出这个问题，其余的事由我来办。
It's not difficult. Put forward this issue in the face of your courtiers. Leave the rest alone for me.

好！就依夫子。
Ok, I'll do as master told me.

十几天后
More than ten days later

夫子,今天我办了一件大好事!
Master, I did a great thing today.

哦!什么好事?
Oh, what's it?

我说通了季桓子,让子羔做了费邑宰。
I persuaded Ji Huanzi to make Zigao governor of Fei.

子路啊,你认为你坠毁郈城 消灭了公孙不狃就了不得啦!
Zilu, do you think you're great after destroying City Hou and getting rid of Gongsun Buniu?

怎么能这样做事?毛毛糙糙,欠考虑!
How can you do this? Careless and thoughtless.

夫子,您不经常教育我们说"人无远虑,必有近忧"吗?
Master, don't you always tell us that people who do not think far ahead will inevitably have worries near at hand.

我让子羔出任费邑宰,也是从长远考虑的。
I am thinking far ahead by making Zigao governor of Fei.

一来我们是同门弟子，将来在官场上好相互有个照应，二来对子羔的前途着想啊！
On one hand, he's my classmate and we can take care of each other at the court.
On the other, I am thinking about Zigao's future.

瞎说！你这是误人子弟！
Nonsense. You're doing harm to others.

误人子弟？我不明白。
Harm him? I don't understand.

费邑有正等着治理的百姓和等待祭祀的社稷，难道一定要读书才算有学问吗？
There are people who are waiting to be governed and imperial divine temple to be worshipped. Won't one learned only by reading?

你也经常教育我们学问必须和实践经验相配合，这样不正好锻炼他吗？
You often teach us knowledge must be combined with practice. Isn't this practice to him?

是啊，子羔无论从人品和修养出仕都没有问题。
Yes, Zigao is nice to be governor whether on personality or cultivation.
可他年龄还小，学识和经验方面都还不成熟，他还需要学习。
But he's young, and not mature in knowledge or experience. He needs to learn more.
他现在这样怎么能治理那复杂紊乱的费邑呢？
How can he govern the mess of City Fei now?
你这不是误人子弟又是什么？
If it's not harming others, what's it?

反正我是出于好意。
I'm out of good intention.

我讨厌狡辩的人！好好想想你说过的话和做过的事吧！
I hate persons with bad excuses. Think over what you said and what you did.

■ 子路使子羔为费宰。子曰："贼夫人之子。"子路曰："有民人焉，有社稷焉，何必读书，然为学？"子曰："是故恶夫佞者。"
Zilu made Zigao governor of Fei. Confucius said, You did him harm. Zilu said, There are people need him to govern and imperial divine temple need him to worship. Isn't one learned by reading only? Confucius said, So I hate persons with bad excuses.

译：子路要子羔做费地方的官长。孔子说，"害了人家孩子。"子路说，"有老百姓，有土地庄稼，何必一定读书，才算学问？"孔子说，"所以我讨厌狡辩的人。"

其身正 不令而行

If the Ruler is Personally Upright, All Will Go Well Even Without His Orders

子曰:"其身正,不令而行;其身不正,虽令不从。"——《子路》
Confucius said, If the ruler is personally upright, all will go well even though he does not give orders. But if he is not, even though orders are given, they will not be obeyed. ——Zilu

译:孔子说,"自己行为正当,不发命令也办得通;自己行为不正当,发命令也没人听从。"

子曰:"邦有道,谷;邦无道,谷,耻也。"——《宪问》
Confucius said, If a country has a wise ruler, we can get its salary. If not, Getting its salary is a kind of shame. ——Xianwen

译:孔子说:"政治清明,领薪水,政治不清明,领薪水,这就是耻辱。"

我是齐国使臣，特来献美女、良马于鲁君。
I'm Envoy from Qi, I'm here presenting King of Lu beauties and horses.

请大家给太宰大人让条路，让季大人定夺。
Give way to Taizai, please. Let Minister Ji have a look.

美啊！美若天仙！
Beautiful! They are really out of this world!

人無求應必有近憂 / If the Ruler is Personally Upright, All Will Go Well Even Without His Orders

太宰大人！太宰大人！
Taizai nibs! Taizai nibs!

太宰大人！
Taizai nibs!

有劳使官，有劳使官了。
Thank you so much, Envoy.

下官奉齐君之命，特向您及鲁君献上这八十位美女和一百二十匹良马。
With the order of King of Qi, I present you and King of Lu these 80 beauties and 120 horses.
本该进城送到贵府，可恐大司寇孔丘不允，所以才……
I should have sent it to your mansion. We're afraid Sikou Kongqiu won't allow us to do. So, we…

哼！孔丘？！他有什么权利不允，走，进城！
Oh, Kongqiu, who give him right not to allow? Go, let's enter city.

不过，这些齐女初来贵国，恐怕不懂这里的风俗，依下官之见，还是送到贵府，等太宰调教数日再送鲁君会更好些。
These Qi ladies come to your country for the first time. Know little about your customs here. In my view, send them first to your mansion, It's better to present them to King after a few days' training.

哈哈……哈哈……还是使官想得周到啊，那就先到我府，走，进城！
Haha (laughter). Envoy is so considerate. Ok. Let's come to my mansion first. Go, let's go into the city.

这正合我意，我要美中选优，剩下的再给定公。
Suit me. I can choose the most beautiful ones and present the rest to Dinggong.

季桓子呢？怎么又没来？
Where's Ji Huanzi? Why not coming again?

启禀国君，季桓子称家中有事，没来上朝。
King, he said he had something at home and couldn't go to the court.

我听说齐国送来了美女、良马。
I heard that Qi presented beauties and horses.

一连几日我宣季桓子进宫议事，他竟不赴召，这季桓子也太不把我放在眼里了，齐国的美女明明是送我的。
For several days, I asked Ji Huangzi to discuss affairs at court, he refused to come. He made nothing of me. Qi beauties were presented to me.

退朝，退朝！
Go home. Go home!

啊!
Ah!

不知国君驾临小府,恕罪、恕罪!
Don't know King is coming to my house. Forgive me. Forgive me!

拜见国君!
Good morning, King.

太宰好快活呀!
How happy Taizai is!

齐国小使拜见国君!
Envoy of Qi worship King.

罢了,罢了!我是不需要拜见的!
Ok, ok. There's no need to worship me.

国君息怒，小使受齐君之命，特向您献上八十位美女、一百二十匹良马，以表仰慕之情。
Don't be angry, King. Ordered by King of Qi. I present you 80 beauties and 120 horses to express our admiration.

季太宰怕齐女不懂鲁国风情，特在府中进行调教，以使国君欢心。
Taizai Ji is afraid Qi ladies know little about Lu's customs. He wants to train them well before presenting to you to have fun.

哈哈哈哈……太宰大人做事一向细心周到，不知现在调教的怎样了？
Haha (laughter). Taizai is always thoughtful. How are they trained now?

嘿嘿嘿嘿……有一半已调教好了，正要给您送去。
Heihei. Half of them are prepared and are going to see you.

是，是。
Yes, King.

好吧，一半留在你府继续调教。
Ok. Leave the rest half here to be trained.

子路，最近在季太宰家怎样啊？
Zilu, how are you in Taizai's mansion?

唉，别提啦！自从齐国送来美女，那季桓子和定公根本就不理朝政，
Oh, don't mention it. Since Qi beauties were presented, Ji Huanzi and Dinggong don't handle affairs at all.
日夜轻歌曼舞，和那些美女饮酒作乐。
Dancing and singing, drinking with those beauties, they have fun day and night.
对我也逐渐疏远了，我早就不想干了。
They are getting away from me too. I won't do with them.

他们不理朝政，夫子代理相事，前来拜访的官员络绎不绝，这不正是可以实现您治理国家的愿望吗？
They neglect state affairs. Master is taking the place of prime minister. Officers come to visit us on and on. Can't your wish of governing the country come true now?

事情哪有你想的那么简单呢，无论是国君还是朝政大员，自己的行为要正当，自己正当了，不发令事情也办得通，自己不正当。下了令也没人听从。
It is not so simple as you think. Whether king or minister, he should be personally upright. If he is personally upright, all will go well even though he does not give orders. But if he is not, even though orders are given, they will not be obeyed.

有这样的国君，我就是再努力，国家也不会繁荣强大啊！
With such a king, however hard I work, our country will not be powerful and prosperous.

夫子，您辛苦大半生，好不容易当上了大司寇，现又代理相事，管他国君怎样，还是照拿俸禄，何必忧虑那么多呢？
Master, working hard for half the life, you are Sikou now, and taking the place of prime minister, whatever King do, you will get your salary. Why worry so much?

你这就大错特错了！国家的政治清明，可以吃俸禄，国君的政治不清明，再吃俸禄，那是一种耻辱！
You're absolutely wrong. If a country has a wise ruler, we can get its salary. If not, getting its salary is a kind of shame.

■ 子曰："其身正，不令而行；其身不正，虽令不从。"
Confucius said, If the ruler is personally upright, all will go well even though he does not give orders. But if he is not, even though orders are given, they will not be obeyed.

译：孔子说，"自己行为正当，不发命令也办得通；自己行为不正当，发命令也没人听从。"

■ 子曰："邦有道，谷；邦无道，谷，耻也。"
Confucius said, If a country has a wise ruler, we can get its salary. If not, getting its salary is a kind of shame.

译：孔子说："政治清明，领薪水，政治不清明，领薪水，这就是耻辱。"

听其言而观其行

Listen to What One Says and Watch What He Does

子曰:"始吾于人也,听其言而信其行;今吾于人也,听其言而观其行也。"——《公冶长》

Confucius said, In the past, I believed in what one does after listening to what he says. But now, I listen to what one says and watch what he does.——Gongyechang

译:《孔子》说,"开始我对人,是听他的语言而相信他的行为;如今我对人,是听他的语言,而观察他的行为。"

子曰:"小子何莫学夫诗?诗,可以兴,可以观,可以群,可以怨。迩之事父,远之事君。多识于鸟兽草木之名。"——《阳货》

Confucius said, Boys, why don't you study poems hard? Studying poems can stimulate enthusiasm, improve observation, unite a lot of persons, and express one's negative feelings. You can take care of your parents now and serve the king in the future. You can also know more names of birds and animals.——Yanghuo

译:孔子说,"年轻人为什么不学习《诗经》?诗可以启发想象,可以观察事物,可以会和群体,可以表达哀怨。近用来侍奉父母,远用来侍奉国君,还可以认识和记忆许多动物和植物的名称。"

■ 子曰:"小子何莫学夫诗?诗,可以兴,可以观,可以群,可以怨。迩之事父,远之事君。多识于鸟兽草木之名。"
Confucius said, Boys, why don't you study poems hard? Studying poems can stimulate enthusiasm, improve observation, unite a lot of persons, and express one's negative feelings. You can take care of your parents now and serve the king in the future. You can also know more names of birds and animals.

译:孔子说,"年轻人为什么不学习《诗经》?诗可以启发想象,可以观察事物,可以会和群体,可以表达哀怨。近用来侍奉父母,远用来侍奉国君,还可以认识和记忆许多动物和植物的名称。"

我们牢记夫子的教诲，下功夫学习《诗经》。
We'll keep master's words in mind and study book of poetry hard.

是啊！一定牢记夫子的教诲。
Yes. We will keep in mind.

子贡，拿上这只杯子。到河边，让那位女子给我们取杯水来。
Zigong, bring this cup. Go to the riverside and ask the lady to take us a cup of water

是。
Yes, sir.

啊？！
Ah.

大姐啊，我是北方人，来到你们楚地。
Sister, I come to your place of Chu from the north.
今逢天热，心里也烦躁，请借一杯水喝好吗？
It's hot today and I feel fidgety. Can you bring me a cup of water?

我们阿谷之水，滔滔东流，直入大海。
Our surging Agu River flows east and pours into the sea.
你就随便喝呗，何必问我，又何必言借呢？
Drink yourself. Why do you ask me and why do you say "borrow"?

给我取一杯好吗？
Pick me a cup, ok?

好吧。
Ok.

按照礼节，我不能亲手交给你，请你自己端吧。
I can not give it to you myself according to etiquette. Pick it yourself.

谢谢。
Thank you.

嗯，看来这女子还是很懂礼节的，有教养，有教养啊！
Oh, yes, it seems that that lady has good manner. Well-bred! Accomplished!

啊？！
Ah.

你拿上这把琴,再跑一趟,让她调一调音。
Bring this zither and go to her again. Ask her to tune it.

好的。
Yes, sir.

啊?!
Ah.

哼!又搞什么名堂?这怎能调音?
Oh. What's he doing? How can it be tuned without its shaft?

刚才喝了你的水,如遇甘霖,听了你的话如沐春风,真的好像是他乡遇知音。
You water is like timely rain for me. What you said is so inspiring. I really felt that I came across a bosom friend in another country.

你言重了,小女子不敢当。
Not at all, sir. You flattered me.

我有把琴，调弦的轴没有了，请你给我调调音。
I have a zither here. It has no shaft. Can you tune it for me?

哈哈……我一个乡野女子，见识短浅，孤陋寡闻，不识五音，不要说你的琴没有轴，就是有轴我也不会调啊！
Haha (laughter). I'm only a usual girl from countryside. lacking knowledge and experience, I know little about music. A zither without shaft. Even with shaft, I can not tune.

嗯，如果是遇到贤人，她会表示礼敬的。可是……
Ah. If she meet a person with virtue. She'll show her respect. But…

难道我不是贤人吗？是你让我……
Am not I？You let me…

哈哈……我不是说你不贤。
I don't mean you aren't.

你再跑一趟,把它送给那位女子吧。
Go to her once more. Give this to the lady.

这……
This.

去吧。
Go.

是。
Yes, sir.

夫子，你一而再，再而三地让子贡跑来跑去，是何原因？
Master, you asked Zigong to go to the lady again and again, Why?
是啊，夫子给我们讲讲这其中的道理吧。
Yes, tell me the reason, master.

一来，子贡能言善辩，适合做这种事情，更重要的是我们为了了解这里的风土人情。
For one thing, Zigong has a silver tongue, he's suit for this kind of thing. What's more important for us is to know more about the local color here.

为什么就专找一个人了解呢？
Why do you get it from only one lady?

过去我对人是听了他的话就信了他的行为；现在我对人是听了他的话再看他的行为。
In the past, I believed in what one does after listening to what he says. But now, I listen to what one says and watch what he does.

哦，原来是这样。
Oh. That's it.

■ 子曰："始吾于人也，听其言而信其行；今吾于人也，听其言而观其行也。"

Confucius said, In the past, I believed in what one does after listening to what he says. But now, I listen to what one says and watch what he does.

译：《孔子》说，"开始我对人，是听他的语言而相信他的行为；如今我对人，是听他的语言，而观察他的行为。"

后生可畏

The Younger Generation Will Surpass the Older

子曰:"后生可畏,焉知来者之不今也?四十、五十而无闻焉,斯亦不足畏也已!" ——《子罕》

Confucius said, The young generation are always better than the elder. How do you know the newcomers are not as good as us? If one person is unknown at his forties or fifties, he will not be respected any longer. ——ZiHan

译:孔子说,"年轻人是可敬畏呀,怎么能认为后来的不如今天的人呢?一个人到了四十岁五十岁还不明白道理,那就不值得敬畏了。"

子曰:"三人行,必有我师焉,择其善者而从之,其不善者而改之。"
——《述而》

Confucius said, One out of three must be our teacher. Learn his good qualities from him and get away his shortcomings from us. ——Shuer

译:孔子说,"三个人一起走路,一定有值得我学习的老师。选择他的优点而学习,看到他的短处而改正自己。"

大家看，这里山川秀丽，土地肥沃，庄稼茂盛，纪障真是个好地方，果然名不虚传。
Look around you, beautiful mountains and rivers, fertile land, lush crops, Jizhang is really a terrific place.

来人了，来人了，快躲开吧！
They are coming. Hurry to stand aside.

为什么要躲？看我的。
Why stand aside? Look at me.

无知小儿为什么挡路？快躲开！
Ignorant kids, get away from here, why are you in our way?

子路，休得无理！
Zilu, don't be impolite.

你小小年纪，为何在路中央挡道？
You're so young, why do you stand in the middle of the way?

我哪里是在路中央？分明是在城中！
I'm not in the middle of the way, I'm obviously in the middle of a town.

哦？城在何处？
Oh, where's the town?

就在脚下！
It's just under your feet.

你筑这城有什么用？
What's the town for?

抵御敌方的车马军队！
Defend the enemies' carts, horses and army.

敢问夫子，车马遇城，是城躲车呢还是车躲城？
May I ask: should town stands aside from carts or carts from town?

哦！小小年纪，竟然能想到这些？在众人面前又是不卑不亢，神童，神童啊！
Oh! Think of these at such an early age, so supercilious in public and you're really a prodigy, a prodigy.

■ 子曰:"后生可畏,焉知来者之不今也?四十、五十而无闻焉,斯亦不足畏也已!"

Confucius said, The young generation are always better than the elder. How do you know the newcomers are not as good as us? If one person is unknown at his forties or fifties, he will not be respected any longer.

译:孔子说,"年轻人是可敬畏呀,怎么能认为后来的不如今天的人呢?一个人到了四十岁五十岁还不明白道理,那就不值得敬畏了。"

《论语》名句故事

都说这里人聪明过人，我倒要看看他们有多聪明。
It's said that the people here were cleverer than others, I want to see how clever they are.
喂！农家大哥，过来问你个事情。
Hello. Brother, come here, I want to ask you about somthing

你这是干的什么农活？
What kind of farm work do you do?
锄地啊！
Hoeing.
我看你忙忙碌碌在田里劳作，你这锄头一天要抬多少次啊？
You're busy working in the field. How many times do you pick up every day?

这个，这……
This, this.

哈哈……
haha.

我父锄地，自然知道一天要抬多少次。
Dad does hoeing. He surely knows how many times he picks up a day.

110

我看夫子出行必坐车，我想你该知道你的马一天抬多少次蹄子吧？
Confucius travels by cart, you must know how many times your horses make steps.
呵呵，童子果然聪颖机敏。
Hehe. You’re really smart.
你我各出题，相互应对，胜者为师如何？
I suggest we each put forward a question for the other to answer. The winner will be the teacher, ok?
可以，不可戏言。
All right. Do not joke.
一言为定。
it's a deal.
你出的主意，你先出题吧.
Your idea, you first.
好,我先出。
Ok, I begin.
人生于世，皆托日月星辰之光，地生五谷杂粮滋养众生，
For the light of the sun, the moon and all the stars, for different kind of grains grow in the field, we can live in this world.
请问童子，天上有多少星星？地上有多少五谷？
Kid, please tell me: How many stars are there in the sky, and how many grains are there in the field?
天高不能上去，地广不能丈量，这……
The sky is too high to climb up, and the field is too wide to measure, this…

哈哈……
haha.

无知小儿，快快下跪拜师吧！哈哈……
Ignorant kid, hurry to kneel down before your master.

哈哈，你们还真以为我答不出来？耍耍你们而已。
Haha. You really believe I can't answer this question? I just play tricks on you.

听着，天上有一夜的星星，地上一年有一茬五谷。
Listen, there are a night's stars in the sky. There are a crop of grains in the field a year.

啊！哈哈
Ah. Ha ha

该我出题了
My turn.

请问夫子，鹅鸭为什么能浮在水面上？
My question is: Why can geese and ducks be on the water?

雁鹤为什么善于鸣叫？
Why are wild geese and cranes good at singing？

松柏为什么冬夏常青？
Why are pines and cypresses evergreen both in winter and summer？

鹅鸭能浮在水面上，是因为它们的脚是方的；雁鹤善于鸣叫是因为它们的脖子长；松柏冬夏常青，是因为树心坚实。

Because of their square feet, Geese and ducks can float on water. Because of their long necks, wild geese and cranes are good at singing, because of their solid heart, pines and cypresses are evergreen both in summer and winter.

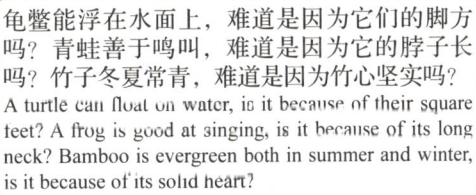

对，对啊。
Right, right.

对什么对，不对！
Why right. Wrong.

龟鳖能浮在水面上，难道是因为它们的脚方吗？青蛙善于鸣叫，难道是因为它的脖子长吗？竹子冬夏常青，难道是因为竹心坚实吗？

A turtle can float on water, is it because of their square feet? A frog is good at singing, is it because of its long neck? Bamboo is evergreen both in summer and winter, is it because of its solid heart?

聪明过人，知识渊博，项橐虽幼，可以为师，可以为师啊！

Smarter than common and knowledgeable. Although young. Xiang Tuo can be my teacher, my teacher.

啊？
Ah.

哈哈哈哈！
Ha ha ha.
嘿！
Hey！

正要拜师，你为何入水？
I'm going to formally acknowledge you as my master. Why do you jump into water?

依礼，沐浴后才可拜啊！夫子也来沐浴吧？
In accordance with the rites, we only acknowledge master after bath, right? Come and bath, Confucius.

我没学过游水，恐怕沉入水底。
I haven't learned how to swim, I'm afraid to be drowned.

学一学鸭子凫水啊。
Learn from ducks how to float on water.

哦，对了，适才说鹅鸭脚方不对，是因为鹅鸭有离水之毛，所以它们不会下沉。
Oh, by the way, what I said a moment ago is wrong. Geese and ducks can float on water because of their feather that out of water.

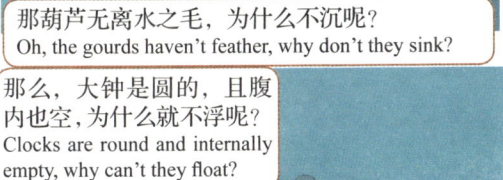

那葫芦无离水之毛，为什么不沉呢？
Oh, the gourds haven't feather, why don't they sink?

葫芦因为腹内空，故而不沉。
Gourds float because they are internally empty,.

那么，大钟是圆的，且腹内也空，为什么就不浮呢？
Clocks are round and internally empty, why can't they float?

这，这……
This, this.

夫子，不要理这傲慢无理的顽童，我们赶路吧。
Master. Don't talk to this arrogant urchin, let's hurry forward.

君子之约，童叟无欺。
A gentlemen's covenant deceits nobody either kids or seniors.
快去设案，等他上来行拜师之礼。
Go to set the table. I'll wait for him and formally acknowledge him as my master.

还要真拜啊？不能拜，对，不能拜！
Are you serious? You can't. Right, you can't.

大家听着，三个人同行，其中必定有人可以做我的老师。要选择他好的方面向他学习，看到他不好的地方，就对照自己改正自身的缺点。
listen, everyone, one out of three must be my teacher. We should learn good aspects from him. For his shortcomings, we must see if we have the same and try to correct them.

■ 子曰："三人行，必有我师焉，择其善者而从之，其不善者而改之。"
Confucius said, One out of three must be our teacher. Learn his good qualities from him and get away his shortcomings from us.

译：孔子说，"三个人一起走路，一定有值得我学习的老师。选择他的优点而学习，看到他的短处而改正自己。"

子见南子

Confucius Meeting with Nanzi

子见南子，子路不说〔悦〕。夫子矢之曰："予所否者，天厌之！天厌之！"——《雍也》

Confucius met with Nanzi, Zilu was angry. Confucius said to him, If I did wrong, God will tire of me! God will tire of me! ——Yongye

译：孔子拜会了南子，子路不高兴。孔子发誓说，"我如果做了错事，老天会惩罚我！老天会惩罚我！"

子曰："吾未见好德如好色者也。"——《子罕》

Confucius said, I have never seen a man who is fond of virtue more than women.
——Zihan

译：孔子说，"我没有看见喜爱道德能像喜爱女色这样的人啊。"

打扰夫子了，南子夫人再次要召见您。
Sorry to interrupt you, master. Ms. Nanzi wants to see you again.

去，去……上次不去，这次也不去！快走吧！
Go away! Leave! Didn't go last time. Won't go now！leave quickly！

子路，休得无礼！
Zilu, don't be rude.

请上官带路，孔丘去见夫人。
Lead the way, please. Kongqiu will go to see her.

请！
Please.

夫子怎么能单独去见这样的女人呢？
How can master see this kind of woman alone?

师兄，南子究竟是什么样的女人？听说她长得很美。
Brother, what kind of woman is Nanzi? I heard that she's very beautiful.

《论语》名句故事

呸！这南子纯粹就一个放荡不羁的淫妇！
Bah, Nanzi is an unconventional and uninhibited bad woman.

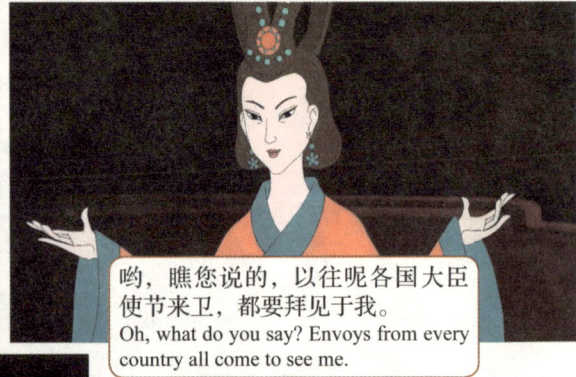

孔丘拜见夫人！
Kongqiu worship madam.

夫子免礼，小女子回礼了！
No salutation, master. I repay a salutation.

能得夫人召见，孔丘深感荣幸。
It' a great honour to see you, madam.

哟，瞧您说的，以往呢各国大臣使节来卫，都要拜见于我。
Oh, what do you say? Envoys from every country all come to see me.

嘿，嘿……你就不同了 请都请不来。
Heihei (laughter), you're different. I invited you several times.
今天能见到当今声名远扬的大圣人，小女子才荣幸！
I'm really honored to see you, a well-known sage.
我听说夫子博学多识，很想请教一二。
I heard that master is well-learned. I'd like to ask you for some advice.

孔丘不是什么圣人，实乃一普通之人。夫人贵体，不能劳累；再者，还有弟子等我，夫人如果没其它事情，孔丘告辞了。
Kongqiu is not a sage but a common man. Madam can't be tired. And my students are all waiting for me. If there's no other thing, I'll say good bye.

事倒是没有，就是……
No other thing, just…

就是什么？
Just what?

就是想跟夫子聊聊天，哈哈……夫子，你看我美吗？
I just want to chat with master. Haha (laughter). Look, am I beautiful?

夫人，恕孔丘失礼，告辞！
Madam, forgive me. Good bye.

迂腐，不识抬举，哼！
Pedantic, don't know how to appreciate favors.

夫子回来了。
Master's coming back.

回来了。
Yes.

见到南子了？
See Nanzi?

见到了。
Yes.

我去见南子是不得已而为之啊。
I did it against my will.

一来她多次召见，二来她贵为国君夫人，依礼答谢也是人之常情。
For one thing, she invited several times. For the other, she's wife of the king. It's common sense to thank her.

她虽然贵为国君夫人，但这种臭名远扬、生活淫乱的女人，根本就不值得您去拜见，您要珍惜自己的名声啊！
Although she's king's wife, she's unconventional and uninhibited bad woman. She's not worthy of your visit. Cherish your fame, please.

我去见南子，如果做了错事，上天就会厌弃我！上天就会厌弃我啊！
I went to meet Nanzi. If I did wrong, God will tire of me! God will tire of me!

■ 子见南子，子路不说（悦）。夫子矢之曰："予所否者，天厌之！天厌之！"
Confucius met with Nanzi, Zilu was angry. Confucius said to him, if I did wrong, God will tire of me! God will tire of me!

译：孔子拜会了南子，子路不高兴。孔子发誓说，"我如果做了错事，老天会惩罚我！老天会惩罚我！"

君王啊，我有个主意能使你的威望大大提升，嘻嘻……
King, I've an idea to promote your prestige. Xixi (laughter).

哦？！夫人有什么好主意，说来给我听。
Oh, what good idea does my dear have? Tell me.

那孔丘乃当今圣人，在各国都有很高的威望。
Kongqiu is a sage of today. He enjoys high prestige all over the world.

现在他在我们国家，我们何不借他的威望张扬一下我们的名声呢？
Now he's in our country. Why not improve our fame by his prestige?

好！好主意！
Good, good idea.

这，这……
This, this.

夫子请吧！该出发了。
Come on, master. It's time to set off.

请吧！
Please.

啊？怎么能这样？太不尊重夫子了吧！
Ah! How can they do this? Don't respect master at all!

唉……
Ah.

出发！
Set off!

看那个就是大名鼎鼎的孔夫子。
Look! That's the well-known Confucius.

哦！孔夫子。
Oh, Confucius!

他怎么能跟宦官同乘一辆车？
How is he in the same carriage with eunuchs?

太不像话了！
What a shame!

太不像话了！
What a shame!

《论语》名句故事

> 那卫灵公真是个混账东西！根本没有把夫子当回事！
> Wei Linggong is really a bastard. He pays no attention to our master.

> 失礼，失礼！简直就是无礼！
> Impolite! Absolutely rude!

> 唉！我没有见过喜爱道德就像喜爱女色那样的人那？
> Hey. I have never seen a man who is fond of virtue more than women.

■ 子曰："吾未见好德如好色者也。"
Confucius said, I have never seen a man who is fond of virtue more than women.

译：孔子说，"我没有看见喜爱道德能像喜爱女色这样的人啊。"

道不同不相为谋

**No Common Goal,
No Planning Together**

子曰:"道不同,不相为谋。"——《卫灵公》
Confucius said, No common goal, no planning together. ——Weilinggong

译:孔子说,"所走的路不同,就不必相互商量谋划事情。"

子曰:"名不正,则言不顺;言不顺,则事不成;事不成,则礼乐不兴;礼乐不兴,则刑罚不中;刑罚不中,则民无所措手足。"——《子路》
Confucius said, If terminology is not corrected, what is said cannot be followed. If what is said cannot be followed, work cannot be accomplished. If work cannot be accomplished, ritual and music cannot be developed. If ritual and music cannot be developed, criminal punishments will not be appropriate. If criminal punishments are not appropriate, the people cannot make a move. ——Zilu

译:孔子说,"如果名不正,说话就不顺当;说话不顺当,就搞不成事情;搞不成事情,礼乐就复兴不起来;礼乐不复兴,刑罚就不会恰当;刑罚不恰当,老百姓就不知道应该如何行为、活动。"

加鞭快行吧,我们尽快赶到卫国城帝丘。
Speed up! Let's get to Diqiu, capital of Wei as soon as possible.

是!驾!
Yes, sir. Quick!

孔丘惊扰灵公了!
Sorry to disturb Linggong!

夫子学识广博,声名远扬,能来卫国,实乃荣幸,也是卫国之福啊!
Master is well-learned and well-known. It's a great honour to have you here in Wei. It's also good luck of Wei.

灵公过奖了。
Linggong flattered me.

夫子一路劳顿,进宫叙话吧!
You must be tired after a long journey. Let's come into the palace to have a talk.

夫子初来卫国 感觉如何？ Master has just arrived. How do you feel about Wei?	卫国人口众多，国泰民安！ With a big population, Wei is prosperous and the people live in peace.
和你鲁国相比如何？ How is it compare with Lu?	鲁卫兄弟也！ Lu and Wei are brother countries.
不知夫子在鲁俸粟几何？ I wonder how much millet you got from Lu as a salary?	俸粟六万。 60,000.
好，寡人也给你俸粟六万。 Ok, I give you 60,000, too.	谢灵公！ Thank you. Linggong!

退朝吧！以后我们再慢慢请教夫子。
That's all for today's court. We'll ask for your advice later.

是，是。
Ah.

我们跟随夫子来卫，难道是为这六万俸粟而来吗？
Following Master to Wei, are we for this 60,000?
来到这里，连住处也不给我们安排，难道这就是他们的待客之道吗？
We aren't accommodated here. Is it their way of treat guests?

夫子如不嫌弃，就暂住到寒舍吧。
Master, if you don't mind, please come to my place to live.

也许灵公一时没顾上安排我们的住处，那就只好打扰颜大夫了！
Maybe Linggong forgot our dwelling place in a hurry. Then we will trouble Dafu Yan for a while.
夫子能住小府，荣幸之至，荣幸之至啊！
It's a great honour to me for you living at my home.

数月以后
A few months later

不知弥大夫驾到，有失远迎，失礼，失礼！
Not knowing your coming to visit me. Sorry for not welcome you earlier.

夫子客气。早该拜访，无奈国事缠身。
Master is over polite. I should have visited you earlier, but I am troubled by national affairs.

今来拜访，一是为了看望夫子，二是想请夫子出山做事。
My visit today, on one hand, I want to see Master; on the other, I'd like to invite you to do things.

哦！？大夫是受灵公之命吗？不知要让我做何事。
Oh, you are ordered by Linggong, aren't you? What kind of things?

夫子来卫已有数月，我多次奏明国君，
You've been in Wei for several months. I asked the king over and over.
可灵公根本就没打算启用您。
But Linggong didn't plan to use you.
夫子博学，不用岂不浪费，倒不如来我府上，早晚便于请教。
Master is so learned, it's really a waste if not be used. Why not come to my mansion in order that I can ask for your advice day or night?

既然国君无此打算，我身边还有这许多弟子，实在对不起弥大夫了！
Since the king has no intention, and I have all these students here, I have to say sorry to Dafu Mi.

既然夫子到我府感觉屈就，那您就等国君的好消息吧。
Since you are not satisfied with my offer, wait for good news from the King.

夫子，我们已来数月，那灵公不理不睬，
Master, we have been here for several months. Linggong leave us alone here.
您还不如到弥子暇门下，他可是卫国重臣，
It's better to accept Mi Zixia's offer. He's the most important minister of Wei.
在他门下，也许能实现您的价值和理想。
With him, perhaps you can make good use of yourself and realize your dream.

子路，你糊涂啊！
Zilu, how silly you are!

请夫子指教。
Your advice, master.

弥子暇再是位高权重，我投他门下，则是名不正言不顺。
Though Mi Zixia is in high position, with him, my terminology is not corrected.
如果名不正，说话就不顺当；说话就不顺当，就搞不成事情；
if terminology is not corrected, what is said cannot be followed. If what is said cannot be followed, work cannot be accomplished.
搞不成事情，礼乐就复兴不起来；
If work cannot be accomplished, ritual and music cannot be developed.
礼乐不复兴，刑罚就不会恰当。
If ritual and music cannot be developed, criminal punishments will not be appropriate.
刑罚不恰当 老百姓就不知道应该如何行为和活动。
If criminal punishments are not appropriate, the people cannot make a move.
这是不能有一点随便和马虎的。
No carelessness will be allowed on this.

■ 子曰："名不正，则言不顺；言不顺，则事不成；事不成，则礼乐不兴；礼乐不兴，则刑罚不中；刑罚不中，则民无所措手足。"

Confucius said, If terminology is not corrected, what is said cannot be followed. If what is said cannot be followed, work cannot be accomplished. If work cannot be accomplished, ritual and music cannot be developed. If ritual and music cannot be developed, criminal punishments will not be appropriate. If criminal punishments are not appropriate, the people cannot make a move.

译：孔子说，"如果名不正，说话就不顺当；说话不顺当，就搞不成事情；搞不成事情，礼乐就复兴不起来；礼乐不复兴，刑罚就不会恰当；刑罚不恰当，老百姓就不知道应该如何行为、活动。"

夫子，我知错了。我会牢记您的教导。
Master, I know I'm wrong. I'll keep your instruction in mind.
我们都会牢记的。
We'll too.

孔老夫子，国君请您进宫。
Confucius, our king invites you to the court.

哦？！请我进宫。好，好，我们走吧。
Oh, to the court. Ok, let's go.

看来夫子的机会来了！
It seems that master's time is coming.
是啊，快一年了，我们的夫子终于等到了机会。
Yes, wait for nearly one year, our master finally got his chance.

拜见国君。
Good morning, king.

谢座！
Thank you.

夫子免礼，免礼！赐座！
Master, don't be so polite. Seated please.

不知君王招孔丘何事？
What do you meet me for?

《论语》名句故事

夫子来卫近一年了，国事繁忙，照顾不周。
You've been in Wei for nearly one year. National affairs trouble me so much. Sorry for the poor service.

君王客气！
King, you are over polite.

不知俸粟够不够用？
Is salary enough?

足矣！
Enough.

卫齐联盟，和晋国征战多年，请问夫子军队该怎样列阵，怎样才能打胜仗呢？
The union of Wei and Qi fighting with Jing for many years. Do you have any ideas of how to make battle arrays to win the war, master?

君王，礼节仪式方面的事，我曾听说一些，这军队作战方面的事嘛……我没学过。
King, I heard of something about courtesy and etiquette. But I have never leaned anything about fight and war.

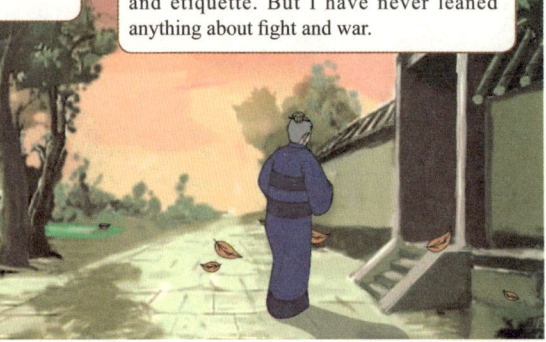

道不同不相为谋 *No Common Goal, No Planning Together*

夫子回来了。
Master is coming back.

夫子，卫灵公给您个什么官？
Master, what position did Wei Linggong offer you?

唉——，所走的路不同，就不必相互商量谋划事情了。
Oh. No common goal, no planning together.

夫子，怎么啦？
Master, what's wrong?

怎么啦？
What's up?

看来卫国并非我们的理想之地，收拾一下行囊，明天离开这里。
It seems that Wei is not our ideal place. Pack up. Let's leave here tomorrow.

■ 子曰："道不同，不相为谋。"
　　Confucius said, No common goal, no planning together.

　译：孔子说，"所走的路不同，就不必相互商量谋划事情。"

四海之内皆兄弟

All Men are Brothers Wherever They Come from

子夏曰:"君子敬而无失,与人恭而有礼。四海之内,皆兄弟也。"
——《颜渊》

Zixia said, Gentlemen respect others without loss, get along well with others politely. All men are brothers wherever they come from.——Yanyuan

译:子夏说,"做一个君子,严谨而不放纵,对待别人恭敬而合乎礼制,到处都可以是兄弟"。

子曰:"天生德于予,桓魋其如予何?"——《述而》

Confucius said, Virtue was born to me. What Huan Tui can do with me?——Shuer

译:孔子说,"上天给了我品德,桓魋能对我怎么样?"

好了，大家可以讨论了。
Ok, time for discussion.

老师，宋景公能接纳我们并采纳您的施政主张吗？
Master, can King Song Jinggong accept us and adopt your policy?

会的，会的，我与景公乃同宗同族。且宋又是弱小之国，他没有不想强盛的道理。
Yes, he will. He and I are clansmen. And Song is also a small and powerless kingdom.

可我们的拜见文简都送去三天了，怎还不见来请啊？
But our say hello letter was passed three days ago. Why don't he invite us to meet?
莫急，莫急呀。
Don't worry, don't worry.

我，我也与哥哥捎去家书，让他劝说国君接纳我们。
I, I also sent a letter to my elder brother. Asked him to persuade the king to accept us.

你哥哥，你哥哥是谁呀？他能劝说宋景公？
Who's your brother? Can he?

我哥哥叫桓魋，是宋国大司马呢。
My brother is Huan Tui. He's the greatest general of Song.

啊？！
Ah.

大家耐心等待，继续学习吧
Be patient, go on studying.

有朋自远方来，不亦乐乎。
Friends come from afar. How happy it is!

有人自远方来，不亦烦乎。
Friends come from afar, How troublesome it is!

有人自远方来，不亦烦乎。
Friends come from afar, How troublesome it is!

先生们，你们要干什么？不要打扰我们学习。
Sir, what're you doing here, don't interrupt us.

嘿嘿，我们也来学习啊！
Hei hei, we're here for studying.

请你们离开,不要打扰我们学习。
Get away, don't interrupt us.

大家安静,我们继续学习。
Be quiet, let's go on studying.

有人自远方来,不亦烦乎!
Friends come from afar, How troublesome it is!

让你们学习,让你们学习。
Study? Let you study.

啊?!
Ah.

你们太无礼了,怎么能这样?
You're too rude. How can you?

我们无礼了,你能把我们怎么样啊?
We're rude. How are you going to treat us?

哪里来的贼人，敢到我宋国来捣乱，给我拿下，格杀勿论！
Where are these thieves from? How dare you come to Song to make trouble? Catch them and kill them all.

杀，杀，杀，杀……
Kill, kill, kill, kill

杀啊！
Kill.

嘿嘿，哥哥，您是受景公之命来接我们进宫的吧？
Hei hei, brother, you must come to welcome us with Jinggong's order, right?

这帮无礼之徒啊……
These persons are rude to us…

哼！我是说你们这帮贼人！
Hum, I say you're thieves.

哥哥，我不是已给你捎去家书了吗？我们是来帮助宋国的，不是什么贼人。
Brother, haven't you got my letter? We aren't thieves, we're here to help Song.

四海之内皆兄弟 *All Men are Brothers Wherever They Come from*

你给我滚开！
Get out of my way.

老师，看来宋国非是我们的久留之地，还是快快离开吧！
Master, it's not a good place to stay. Let's go away soon.

天降大任于我，桓魋他怎能奈何于我？
It's me who is determined to shoulder this greatest task. How can Huan Tui do to me?
收拾行囊、车马，离开吧。
Be ready to leave now!

司马牛，你哭什么？是不愿意离开宋国，离开哥哥吗？
Why are you crying, Sima Niu? You are not willing to leave kingdom Song, leave your brother, right?

不是，不是，师兄。我怎么偏偏有这么一个不仁不义的哥哥，凌驾于国君之上，祸害国民。
No, no, brother. Why do I have such a wicked brother? He shows no respect to the king and does evils to the people.
这次又让老师及众师兄蒙受了屈辱。
What's more, he insulted our master and brothers.
我有何颜面面对老师和师兄啊！
I'm really shameful. How can I face the master and all the brothers?

■ 子曰："天生德于予，桓魋其如予何？"
Confucius said, Virtue was born to me. What Huan Tui can do with me?

译：孔子说，"上天给了我品德，桓魋能对我怎么样？"

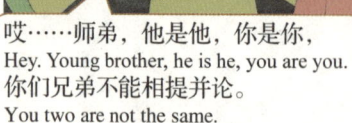

哎……师弟，他是他，你是你，
Hey. Young brother, he is he, you are you.
你们兄弟不能相提并论。
You two are not the same.

你看，我和子贡来自魏国，子石来自楚国，子张来自陈国，你来自宋国，子路和更多的同学来自鲁国。
You see, Zigong and I come from Kingdom Wei, Zishi is from Kingdom Chu, Zizhang is from Chen, You're from Song, Zilu and more other brothers are from Lu.

我们都是来自五湖四海跟随着老师，我们就像是一家人。
From all over the world, following the same master, we are like a big family.
老师不是教导我们：严肃认真的办好每一件事，接人待物恭敬而又合乎礼仪，做这样的人，与这样的人相处，到处都有你的好兄弟，人人都是你的好兄弟。
The master tells us, do every thing carefully, get along with others politely. Be such kind of person, deal with such kind of persons. All men are brothers wherever they come from. And everybody is your good brother.

你何愁没有兄弟呢？
Don't worry that you have no brother.

■ 子夏曰："君子敬而无失，与人恭而有礼。四海之内，皆兄弟也。"
Zixia said, Gentlemen respect others without loss, get along well with others politely. All men are brothers wherever they come from.

译：子夏说，"做一个君子，严谨而不放纵，对待别人恭敬而合乎礼制，到处都可以是兄弟。"

在陈绝粮

Running out of Food When in Chen

在陈绝粮,从者病,莫能兴。子路愠见曰:"君子亦有穷乎?"子曰:"君子固穷,小人穷斯滥矣。"——《卫灵公》

When in Chen, they are running out of food. Some of the followers were ill and couldn't re-collect. Zilu was sad and asked, Master, has gentlemen ever been poor? Confucius said, Gentlemen are surely poor. Aren't we so? But when gentlemen are poor, they can do their duties. While petty men are different. When they are poor, petty men will do evils as they like.——Weilinggong

译:孔子在陈国断了粮食,跟随的人都病了,爬不起来,子路很生气地来见孔子说,"君子也有毫无办法的时候?"孔子说,"君子在没办法的时候,仍然坚持着,小人没办法就胡来了。"

子曰:"贤哉,回也!一箪食,一瓢饮,在陋巷,人不堪其忧,回也不改其乐。贤哉,回也!"——《雍也》

Confucius said, You're really of virtue, Yanhui. For so many years, with a box of rice, a spoon of water, he lived in the old lane. Others can not suffer the sadness. But Yan hui doesn't change his happiness. Really of virtue, Yan Hui! —— Yongye

译:孔子说,"真有贤德啊,颜回。一盒饭,一瓢水,住在破巷子里,别人禁受不住那忧愁,颜回却不改变他的快乐。真有贤德啊,颜回。"

夫子，我们马上要出陈国了，再向前走就到蔡国了。天色已晚，我们就在这里过夜休息吧。
Master, we'll be out of Chen and in Cai soon. It's late. We'll stay here for the night.

好吧，就在这里过夜。
Ok, stop here for the night.

夫子。
Master.

夫子你看，我们被包围了！
Master, look, we're surrounded.

啊？！
Ah？！

这是哪国的军队？他们要干什么？他们要干什么？
Which army is this? What are they going to do? What are they going to do?

大家莫慌乱，子路、公良儒更不要鲁莽，我们等等看。颜回埋锅造饭，饭后我们学习。
Be calm, Zilu, Gong Liangru, you two don't be rash, let's wait and see. Yan hui, cook now, we'll study after meal.

什么人？
Who are you?

军爷，我是孔夫子的学生子贡。请问你们是哪国军队？为什么要围困我们？
Officer, I'm Zigong, a student of Confucius. May I ask which country are you from? Who do you besiege us?

实不相瞒，我们是陈蔡两国的军队。
Tell you the truth, we're army from Chen and Cai.

军爷，请问为什么要围困我们？
Officer, why do you besiege us?

这个嘛……军事秘密，无可奉告！
Well, military secret, have nothing to say.

唉，军爷，军爷，我们都是读书人，告诉我们又何妨呢？我们夫子只是想明白一下缘由，也没有要和你们交战的意思。
Oh, officer, officer, we're all learners, what harm is there if you tell us? Our master just wants to know the reason. We won't fight against you.

其实告诉你也无妨。
It's ok. I'll tell you.
你们不是要去楚国吗？上边就是怕你们一旦去了楚国，孔子受到重用，楚国就会变得更加强大，楚国强大我们陈蔡小国首先要被他们吞掉。
Aren't you going to go Chu? They are afraid that once you're in Chu. If Confucius is put into important position, Chu will become stronger. If Chu is strong, small countries like Chen and Cai will first be annexed.

天色已暗，我们不如趁黑夜杀出一条血路，冲出去！
It's dark. How about killing a bloody way out?

不行，他们里三层外三层，漫山遍野全是军队，怎么能冲的出去呢？
No, there are so many people around us. How can we with soldiers all over the mountain and field?
就算你能冲出去，夫子年老体弱，他可怎么办呢？
If you can rush out, master is old and weak, how can he?
再等等吧！
Let's wait.

我们带的粮食只够吃两天，现在只剩一天的了。
Our food can only last for two days. Now only one day's left.

我们以后每日三顿饭改为一顿，其它的可在附近挖些野菜来充饥，大家说好不好？
We'll have one meal a day instead of three. Get some wild vegetables to eat if you're hungry, ok?

好！好！
Ok, ok.

只能这样办了！
This is the only way.

我们现在就去挖野菜。
Let's go to dig wild vegetables.

夫子年龄大了，不能吃野菜，我们首先要保证夫子的一日三餐。
Master is old, can't have wild vegetables. We'll first prepare three meals a day for him.

《论语》名句故事

大家吃饭喽！
Meal's ready.

颜回啊，这段你掌管粮食和做饭，是不是有多吃或偷的行为啊？
Yan Hui, you're in charge of food and cooking recently. Have you ever stolen or had much food?

夫子，自从我们断粮以来，虽然我掌管大家的饮食，可我没有多吃一口饭。
Mater, since our food was run out, although I'm in charge of our meal, I didn't have more, even a mouth of meal.
今天我是比大家多吃了几粒粮，我看到饭上有泥土 怕让夫子吃到了。
I really have several grains of food more than others today. I saw earth on the meal. I'm afraid master would eat it.
把沾有泥土的饭扔了又可惜，我就吃了。
But it would be a pity if threw it away, so I ate.

呵呵，真有贤德啊，颜回。
Haha (laughter), you're really of virtue, Yanhui.

多少年来，一盒饭，一瓢水，住在破巷子里，别人禁受不住那忧愁，颜回却不改变他的快乐。真有贤德啊，颜回。
For so many years, with a box of rice, a spoon of water, he lived in the old lane. Others can not suffer the sadness. But Yan hui doesn't change his happiness. Really of virtue, Yan Hui!

师弟，师兄错怪你了，对不起！
Brother, I wrong you, sorry.

没什么，师兄。
That's nothing, brother.

■ 子曰："贤哉，回也！一箪食，一瓢饮，在陋巷，人不堪其忧，回也不改其乐。贤哉，回也！"
Confucius said, You're really of virtue, Yanhui. For so many years, with a box of rice, a spoon of water, he lived in the old lane. Others can not suffer the sadness. But Yan hui doesn't change his happiness. Really of virtue, Yan Hui!

译：孔子说，"真有贤德啊，颜回。一盒饭，一瓢水，住在破巷子里，别人禁受不住那忧愁，颜回却不改变他的快乐。真有贤德啊，颜回。"

《论语》名句故事

> 夫子,君子也有穷困的时候吗?
> Master, has gentlemen ever been poor?

> 君子当然也有穷困的时候,我们现在不是这样吗?
> Gentlemen are surely poor. Aren't we so?
> 但是,君子穷困的时候能安守本分,而小人就不同了,小人穷困时就会不顾一切地为非作歹。
> But when gentlemen are poor, they can do their duties. While petty men are different. When they are poor, petty men will do evils as they like.

> 夫子,您说的对。
> Master, you're right.
> 可您看我们现在,饿的饿病的病,不能动的不能动,这样等下去也不是个办法啊?
> But look at us now, either hungry, ill, or can't move. It will not do if we wait like this.

> 是,我看这样吧,明天天不亮趁敌人不备,子贡悄悄出去,向楚国求援。
> Yes. In my view, tomorrow, before dawn, take the enemy unawares. Zigong skips out to ask help from Chu.

> 是。
> Yes.

■ **在陈绝粮,从者病,莫能兴。子路愠见曰:"君子亦有穷乎?"子曰:"君子固穷,小人穷斯滥矣。"**

When in Chen, they are running out of food. Some of the followers were ill and couldn't re-collect. Zilu was sad and asked, Master, has gentlemen ever been poor? Confucius said, Gentlemen are surely poor. Aren't we so? But when gentlemen are poor, they can do their duties. While petty men are different. When they are poor, petty men will do evils as they like.

译:孔子在陈国断了粮食,跟随的人都病了,爬不起来,子路很生气地来见孔子说,"君子也有毫无办法的时候?"孔子说,"君子在没办法的时候,仍然坚持着,小人没办法就胡来了。"

在陈绝粮 Running out of Food When in Chen

子畏于匡

Confucius was Besieged in Kuang

子畏于匡，曰："文王既没，文不在兹乎？天之将丧斯文也，后死者不得与于斯文也；天之未丧斯文也，匡人其如予何？"——《子罕》

Confucius was besieged in Kuang, said, Since King Zhouwen died, I'm the only person who has this culture. If God will destroy this culture, the young generation will know nothing about it. If God is unwilling to destroy this culture, how can Kuang people do with me?——Zihan

译：孔子被囚禁在匡地，说："周文王已经死了，文化不就在我这里了吗？如果上天真要消灭这文化，那么后人也就不会有这文化了。如果上天不愿消灭这文化，匡人又能把我怎么样。"

颜刻，这是什么地方？
Yanke, where is this place?

夫子，这个地方我熟悉，叫匡，原来属于卫国，后来叫郑国占领，现在属于郑国的一个小邑。
Master, I'm familiar here. It's Kuang. It once belonged to Wei. Was occupied by Zheng later. It's now a little city of Zheng.

哦，你对这个地方真的很熟悉啊。
Oh, you're really familiar with this place.

夫子您看那个城墙的缺口，当年我跟随阳虎，就是在那个地方杀进城的。
Look at that gap of the city wall, master. Led by Yanghu that year, I killed my way into the city.

快！守好城门，阳虎又来了，绝不能让他们再进城祸害百姓！
Quick! Guard the city gate carefully. Here comes Yanghu again! We mustn't let them go into the city and harm people.

哪个是阳虎啊？
Who's Yanghu?

车上那个人就是阳虎。
The man on the carriage is.

都给我听好了，要活捉阳虎，为死去百姓报仇！
Listen to me carefully, capture Yanghu alive and avenge those died.

报仇！报仇！报仇！
Revenge! Revenge! Revenge!

是啊，这样下去总不是个办法。要不然我和公良儒打头阵，我们杀出一条血路冲出去，这些小贼根本不在话下。
Yes, we have to find a way. Gong Liangru and I spearhead, let's kill a bloody way out. These thieves are nothing.

夫子，我们带的干粮都吃光了，再这样僵持下去，我们都会困死在这里。
Master, we have no solid food left. In such a stalemate, we'll all die here.

这样不可以，夫子年纪大了，万一有个闪失怎么办？
We can't do that. Since master is old, What if anything go wrong?

是啊，强行向外冲不是个办法。
Yes, it's not a good way to force out.

硬冲不是办法，难道我们在这儿等死不成？
It's not a good way. Shall we wait for death here?

周文王已经死了，文化不就在我这里吗？
Since King Zhouwen died, I'm the only person who has this culture.

如果上天要灭掉这文化，那么后人也就不会有这文化了。
If God will destroy this culture, the young generation will know nothing about it.
如果上天不愿消灭这文化，匡人又能把我怎么样？
If God is unwilling to destroy this culture, how can Kuang people do with me?

我想到了一个办法可以让匡人退。
I have an idea that can make Kuang people retreat.

你？
You ?

■ 子畏于匡，曰："文王既没，文不在兹乎？天之将丧斯文也，后死者不得与于斯文也；天之未丧斯文也，匡人其如予何？"

Confucius was besieged in Kuang, said, Since King Zhouwen died, I'm the only person who has this culture. If God will destroy this culture, the young generation will know nothing about it. If God is unwilling to destroy this culture, how can Kuang people do with me?

译：孔子被囚禁在匡地，说："周文王已经死了，文化不就在我这里了吗？如果上天真要消灭这文化，那么后人也就不会有这文化了。如果上天不愿消灭这文化，匡人又能把我怎么样。"

你们想，匡人把我们当成阳虎等人了，
You think, Kuang people regarded us as Yanghu and his people.
如果我们能找到一个有威望的人来证明我们不是阳虎，他们不就退了吗？
If I can find a big figure to prove we aren't. They will retreat, won't they?

我认为什么好办法呢！在这荒效野外天寒地冻的，匡人又团团围着，上哪儿去找什么有威望的证明人？
What good is it? It's so cold in the field. Being surrounded by Kuang people, where can we find a big figure to prove?

子路莫急，计颜回说说看。
Don't worry, Zilu. Let Yan Hui go ahead.

那天我落在后面，是和一个亲戚说话来，他在宁武子门下当差，我去找他，让宁武子出面，匡人肯定能退。
I fell behind that day because I talked with my relative. He serves for Ning Wuzi. Let me go to find him. Ask Ning Wuzi to show up, Kuang people will surely withdraw.

对，那宁武子是卫国世卿，他肯出面，事情肯定能成。
Yes, Ning Wuzi is the old minister of Wei, if he's willing to, it will be done.

《论语》名句故事

那怎么才能出去找他?
How can we go out for him?

我去试试看。
Let me try.

宁武子拜见夫子，不知夫子受难，恕罪！恕罪！
Ning Wuzi worship master. Not knowing you're suffering here. Sorry. Forgive me.

多谢您的搭救，孔丘有礼了！
I appreciate your help very much. Kongqiu salute to you.

多有得罪，请夫子谅解，恕我们有眼无珠！
Offend you so much. Please forgive us, master. Sorry, we're as blind as bats.

有情可原，大家请起，天冷快快回家吧！
Your case deserves sympathy. Stand up, everyone. It's so cold. Go home quickly.

谢谢夫子！
Thank you, master.

子帅已正 孰敢不正
If the Ruler is Upright Himself, Who Dare not Be?

子曰:"子为政,焉用杀?子欲善而民善矣。君子之德风,人小之德草,草上之风,必偃。"——《颜渊》

Confucius said, Why do you use the way of killing persons to rule the country? First, you have to be upright yourself. If you are upright, the people will be upright. The conduct of officers is like wind and that of common people is like grass. Grass will follow wind. ——Yanyuan

译:孔子说,"你搞政治,为什么要用杀人的办法?你如果想做好人,老百姓也就会跟着好起来。君子的道德像风,老百姓的道德像草,草随风倒。"

子曰:"政者,正也。子帅已正,孰敢不正?"——《颜渊》

Confucius said, Rulers should be upright themselves. If the ruler is upright himself, who dare not be? ——Yanyuan

译:孔子说,"政治就是端正。你率先端正自己,谁敢不端正?"

夫子，我们到家了。
Mater, we're back.

是啊，到家了。十四年了，我孔丘又回来了。
Yes, at home now. 14 years later, Kongqiu come back again.

你是子思吗？都长这么高了。
You must be Zisi, so tall now.

爷爷，爷爷！
Grandfather, grandfather.

哈哈哈哈……走。
Hahaha (laughter), let's go.

爷爷，咱们回家吧。
Grandfather, let's go home.

孔老夫子拜见！
Confucius is asking for a meeting.

孔丘拜见国君！
Kongqiu worship king.

If the Ruler is Upright Himself, Who Dare not Be?

《论语》名句故事

夫子快快请起，您年事已高，何必行此大礼。
Master, stand up quickly. You're so old, why salute me?

夫子请坐。
Take a seat please.

夫子这十几年在外颠沛流离，吃了不少的苦，
Master, having been moving around for ten more years, you must suffered a lot.

我请您回国一是想让您安度晚年，再是国家大事早晚要请教于您。
I ask you to come back to our country, for one thing, I want you to spend your remaining years in happiness. For another, I have national affairs to ask for your advice.

多谢国君重爱，孔丘愿为国家效秉烛之力。
Thanks for your kindness. Kongqiu is willing to devote the rest of my life to our country.

为了您今后的生活，我决定封您为大夫，享受大夫享有的一切俸禄。
I will dub you Dafu for the sake of your life here. You'll be given a salary of Dafu.

多谢国君错爱。
Thank you, king, for your kind offer.

他？他怎么来了？有请。
He, why does he come? Welcome.

夫子，季康子大人来访。
Master, Ji Kangzi come to visit you.

听说夫子回国，特意前来拜访。
Heard that master came back. I come to pay a visit specially.

多谢，多谢！不知太宰大人驾到，有失远迎，望海涵！
Thank you. Not knowing Taizai's coming. Forgive me for not coming early to welcome you.

昨天拜访了国君，正说要去拜访您呢！
I visited king yesterday. I'm about to visit you.

哪里，哪里，国君为上，我区区一人宰怎敢有劳大了。
Oh, no. King comes first. I'm only a Taizai, how dare I trouble master?

哦，不对，应该是孔大夫。
Oh, no. should be Dafu Kong.

这……这……太宰大人请坐！
Well, well. Sit down please, Taizai.

多谢太宰大人！
Thank Taizai.

听说哀公封您为大夫，我封您为国老。
It's said that Aigong dubbed you Dafu. I'll dub you Guolao.

国老就是有职无权的官。
It's a position without power.

国老？国老是个什么官？
Guolao, what kind of officer is it?

孔国老，您弟子三千，在他们中谁最优秀？
Guolao Kong, you have 3,000 students, who is the most excellent?

颜回，可惜他死了。
Yanhui. But it's a pity he died.

您不是说过冉求是"六艺"的尖子，最适合当官吗？
Didn't you say Ranqiu is best at the six arts, and suited for being an officer?

这些年他在我府中 确实展现出了他的智慧和才能．他……
These years he has worked for me. He truly showed his wisdom and talent. He…

他？那是过去。他现在已经不是我的学生了！
He. He was in the past. But now he is not my student.

好了，好了，我们不说冉求，我想请教一下治理国家的大事。
Well, well, we don't talk about Ranqiu any more. I want to ask you some advice on handling national affairs.

哦？请讲！
Oh, go ahead.

现在因为盗贼猖獗，各级官吏也趁机敛财，不止之风盛行。
Now robbery is rampant. All levels of officers take the chance to accumulate wealth. Unhealthy tendencies are prevailing.

我想抓住他们一个个都杀了！主动亲近那些好人，怎么样？
I want to catch them and kill them all, and stay close to those with virtue. How do you think?

你治理国家为什么要用杀人的办法呢？
Why do you use the way of killing persons to rule the country?

首先你必须率先端正自己。
First, you have to be upright yourself.

哦？
Oh？

你端正了，无论是下边官员还是老百姓，谁敢不端正。
If you are upright, Who dare not be whether they are officers or common people?

- 子曰："政者，正也。子帅已正，孰敢不正？"
  Confucius said, Rulers should be upright themselves. If the ruler is upright himself, who dare not be?

  译：孔子说，"政治就是端正。你率先端正自己，谁敢不端正？"

- 子曰："子为政，焉用杀？子欲善，而民善矣。君子之德风，人小之德草，草上之风，必偃。"
  Confucius said, Why do you use the way of killing persons to rule the country? First, you have to be upright yourself. If you are upright, the people will be upright. The conduct of officers is like wind and that of common people is like grass. Grass will follow wind.

  译：孔子说，"你搞政治，为什么要用杀人的办法？你如果想做好人，老百姓也就会跟着好起来。君子的道德像风，老百姓的道德像草，草随风倒。"

学而不厌 诲人不倦
Be Insatiable in Learning and Tireless in Teaching

子曰:"默而识之,学而不厌,诲人不倦,何有于我哉?"——《述而》
Confucius said, Keeping what I saw in mind, studying without satiety, teaching others without weariness. Besides these, what do I have? ——Shuer

译:孔子说,"默记在心,学习而不厌烦,教导别人而不疲倦,我还有什么呢?"

子曰:"君子周而不比,小人比而不周"——《为政》
Confucius said, Gentlemen are good to all people but not partial to someone. Petty men are partial to someone but not good to all. ——Weizheng

译:孔子说,"君子普遍厚待人们,而不偏袒存私;小人偏袒存私,而不普遍厚待。"

陈亢退而喜曰:"问一三得,闻诗,闻礼,又闻君子之远其子也。"
——《季氏》
Chen Kang went back and said happily, One of my questions got three answers. I know the book of poetry and the etiquette, and I also know that gentlemen don't treat their sons specially. ——Jishi

译:陈亢回来后,非常高兴,说,"我问一件事,却知道了三件:知道诗,知道礼,还知道君子不特殊对待自己的儿子。"

《论语》名句故事

子贡师兄！
Brother Zigong.

哦，是子禽呐，你一个人在外面干嘛？
Oh, it's Ziqin. What are you doing alone outside?

哎，心中不快，散散心呗。
Oh, a bit unhappy. Just relax myself.

是不是有人欺负你了？
Put upon by someone?

那倒没有，只是感觉夫子不怎么喜欢我。
No. Just feel that master doesn't like me.

你为什么会这么想？师弟啊，记得有一次夫子当着全体弟子说过，他听到的见到的总是默默地记在心里，对学习从不厌烦，在教育学生方面，却从来不知疲倦，
Why think this way? Brother, I remember master said in the face of all his students, He always kept what he saw in mind silently. He's never tired of studying. He never felt tired in teaching students.

除此以外，其他什么都没有了。
Besides these, he has nothing.

■ 子曰:"默而识之,学而不厌,诲人不倦,何有于我哉?"
Confucius said, Keeping what I saw in mind, studying without satiety, teaching others without weariness. Besides these, what do I have?

译:孔子说,"默记在心,学习而不厌烦,教导别人而不疲倦,我还有什么呢?"

是的,我也记得。
Yes. I remember it too.

可在我看来,师兄您比夫子还要贤明,不过您只是表示对夫子的尊重罢了。
But to me, you are wiser than master. You only show your respect to master.

子禽,我真不知道你哪里来的这古怪想法!
Ziqin, I really don't know why you have this weird idea.

我告诉你,君子说话是不可以不谨慎的
I told you, gentlemen should be guard in their speech.

你只说一句话,别人就可以看出你是聪明还是不聪明。
By one word of you, others will know whether you are smart or not.

我们的夫子是崇高而不可及的,他就好比天一样,无法用梯子爬上去!
No one can be as noble as our master. He's just like the sky. One can not climb up to by a ladder.

《论语》名句故事

> 那夫子是不是只想着当官啊？要不然，他为什么要周游列国啊？
> Master is only thinking of being an officer, isn't he? Otherwise, why does he travel around all the states?

> 夫子周游列国，每到一个国家便和那里的政治发生关系，这究竟是夫子自己去求的，还是人家自动给他的？
> Master travels around, he was always related to the politics there whichever state he arrive in. Did he ask for it himself or others asked him to?

> 给你这样说，如果我们夫子能够掌握一个国家，他不仅能使国家繁荣强大，民众还会从心底里顺从他。
> Put it in this way, if our master can control a country, he can not only make it prosperous and powerful, but also make the people comply with him from the bottom of their heart.

> 他活着，人们讴歌他；他死了，人们会像死去父母一样悲痛。
> People sing the praises of him when he's living. When he passed away, people will feel sad as if their parents died.

> 你想想，我拿什么能和夫子相比？
> Just think, how can I compare with master?

> 听了师兄对夫子的一番宏论，我似乎对夫子和我本人有了一点新的认识。
> Hearing your talk about our master, I seemed to get some new ideas about master and myself.

我认为你不应是"似乎",更不应该是"一点"的问题。那以后就慢慢观察和体悟吧。
It shouldn't be "seem" or "some". Observe and feel slowly yourself.

对!夫子肯定会将私下保留的学问传授给他,我多接触他就是捷径。
Yes, master will surely teach him what he left personally. It will be a shortcut to contact more with him.

观察?
Observe?

伯鱼兄!伯鱼兄!请等一等。
Brother Boyu! Brother Boyu! Wait a moment, please.

嗯,是子禽兄,有事吗?
Oh, it's brother Ziqin. What's it?

没,没,没什么事,想和你聊聊天。
No, nothing. I just want a chat with you.

啊,聊天?好啊。
Ah, chat? Nice.

《论语》名句故事

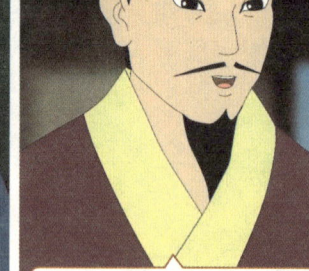

我新来不久,在这里也是人生地不熟的。
I'm new here, a stranger in a strange place.

是不是想家了?
You're homesick, aren't you?

不,不是。我想你是夫子唯一的儿子,肯定接受过不少夫子单独的教诲,学问一定很大,想和你请教一二。
No, no. I think you're the only son of master, you must be taught by him alone, you must be well-learned, I want to ask you for some advice.

其实父亲还从来没有单独对我进行过什么教诲。
In fact, my father never taught me alone.

真的没有?
Really?

噢,有过两次。
Oh, twice.

一天我匆忙走过院子，他正独立在堂上，问我："你开始读诗没有？"
One day, I hurried by the yard, he's standing alone in the hall. He asked me, "Do you start reading poems?"

我说没有，他批评我说："《诗经》上说的事情包罗万象，你不学诗怎能和别人交谈呢？"
I said no. he blamed me, The Book of Poetry is all-embracing. How can you talk with others if you don't study it?

此后，我就认真学诗了。
From then on, I studied the book of poetry hard.

噢，学诗？夫子也公开教导过我们学诗啊。
Oh, study the book of poetry, master told us that in public.

是的，是的，只是我没在意罢了。
Yes, yes. I just didn't care.

还有吗？
Anything else?

还有一次，也是他单独碰到了我，问："你开始学礼了没有？"
Yes. On another occasion, he met me alone. Ask, "Do you start learning etiquette?"

我说没有，他又批评我说："古文化的精髓都在礼上，它可以使人德行坚定，你不学礼，怎么能在社会上立身呢？"
I said no, he blamed me again, The spirit of ancient culture is among the etiqutte, it can make one's virtue more solid. If you don't learn it, how can you conduct yourself in society?

以后我又开始专心学礼。
I start learning etiquette carefully from then on.

还有吗？
Go on.

没有了。
That's all.

夫子好！
Good morning, master.

父亲好！
Good morning, father.

好，好。你们两人好像在院子里谈了很久了，看来很要好嘛。
Hello. It seems that you two have talked for a long time at the yard. You're very close to each other, aren't you?

最近子禽兄经常找我，我们是很亲密的朋友了。
Brother Ziqin often met with me recently. We are close friends.

这是好事啊，年轻人交朋友要相互切磋，相互勉励，不能因你们亲密，对友谊而有所偏失。
Fine. Young men should make friends and study, encourage each other. Your friendship can not be mistaken because you're close.

君子普遍厚待人们，而不偏袒存私；
Gentlemen are good to all people but not partial to someone.

四海之内皆兄弟嘛！你们说对吗？相反，小人就偏袒有私，也不普遍厚待人们。
All men on the earth are brothers. Do you think so? On the contrary, petty men are partial to someone but not good to all.

■ 子曰："君子周而不比，小人比而不周"
Confucius said, Gentlemen are good to all people but not partial to someone. Petty men are partial to someone but not good to all.

译：孔子说，"君子普遍厚待人们，而不偏袒存私；小人偏袒存私，而不普遍厚待。"

是，是。
Yes.

好了，我不打扰了，你们继续聊吧。
Ok, I won't disturb you. Go on with your topic.

《论语》名句故事

> 师弟，好用功啊！
> Brother. How hard you study!

> 师兄，又要出门啊？
> Brother, are you going to go out again?

> 是的，今天精神不错呀，有什么喜事？
> Yes, you're in high spirit today. Any happy things?

> 喜事？也可以说是喜事。
> Happy thing? It is.

> 哦？说来听听。
> Oh, tell me.

> 我更加佩服你了，你说的不假，我们夫子确实伟大！
> I admire you more. You are perfectly right. Our master is really great!

> 我正跟伯鱼说话，正巧碰到了夫子。
> I happened to meet master when I'm talking to Boyu.

> 可以说我是一问三得，知道了诗，知道了礼，还知道了君子不特殊对待自己的儿子。
> Can say one of my questions got three answers. I know the book of poetry and the etiquette, and I also know gentlemen don't treat their sons specially.

■ 陈亢退而喜曰："问一三得，闻诗，闻礼，又闻君子之远其子也。"
Chen Kang went back and said happily, One of my questions got three answers. I know the book of poetry and the etiquette, and I also know that gentlemen don't treat their sons specially.

译：陈亢回来后，非常高兴，说，"我问一件事，却知道了三件：知道诗，知道礼，还知道君子不特殊对待自己的儿子。"